Celebrating the Jewish Holidays

Celebrating the Jewish Holidays

COOKING, CRAFTS, AND TRADITIONS

Sharon Kalman ■ Crafts by Devorah Levinrad ■ Recipes by Anita Hirsch

CRESCENT BOOKS
NEW YORK

A FRIEDMAN GROUP BOOK

This 1992 edition published by Crescent Books, distributed by
Outlet Book Company, Inc., a Random House Company,
225 Park Avenue South, New York, New York 10003.

ISBN 0-517-05180-X

Library of Congress Cataloging-in-Publication Data
    Kalman, Sharon.
        Celebrating the Jewish holidays : cooking, crafts, and customs /
    Sharon Kalman ; crafts by Devorah Levinrad ; recipes by Anita
    Hirsch.
            p.   cm.
        Includes bibliographical references and index.
        ISBN 0-517-05180-X (hardcover)
        1. Fasts and feasts—Judaism.   2. Jewish crafts.   3. Holiday
    decorations.   4. Cookery, Jewish.   I. Levinrad, Devorah.
    II. Hirsch, Anita, M.S.   III. Title.
    BM690.K25   1992
    296.4'3—dc20   91-35887
                                                        CIP

CELEBRATING THE JEWISH HOLIDAYS
Cooking, Crafts, and Traditions
was prepared and produced by
Michael Friedman Publishing Group, Inc.
15 West 26th Street
New York, New York 10010

Editor: Dana Rosen
Art Direction: Devorah Levinrad
Photography Editor: Ede Rothaus

Typeset by Trufont
Color separations by Scantrans Pte. Ltd.
Printed and bound in Hong Kong by Leefung-Asco Printers Ltd.

8   7   6   5   4   3   2   1

The authors wish to thank the Michael Friedman Publishing Group for all of their help and support with this project.

CONTENTS

INTRODUCTION

The Jewish holidays, in addition to being times of religious observance, are also the times for family and friends to gather together to enjoy the stories and foods that make the celebrations memorable. In fact, to many people, the Jewish holidays are defined by a special story, a special food, or a special object that is associated only with that holiday. In *Celebrating the Jewish Holidays* the stories, food, and crafts come together. These chapters are filled with information and ideas about the origin of each holiday, traditional foods, innovative dishes sure to become family favorites, and crafts that run the gamut from Shabbat candlesticks to Rosh Hashanah greeting cards and embroidered *matzah* covers. Once you use this book for one holiday, you will want to use it for every holiday, year after year.

I know that I will never forget spending Passover on a *kibbutz* in Israel, where the words "next year in Jerusalem" took on a special meaning. Here, you will be able to personalize all of the special holidays and festivals, making each one a special time for the entire family.

Whether you are Reformed, Conservative, or Orthodox, whether you live on a kibbutz in Israel or an apartment in Chicago, celebrating the holidays is a way for all Jews to come together, to relive both the tragic and joyful moments in the long history of Judaism. This book will help you and your family get the most from each celebration.

From Shabbat to Passover, Yom Kippur to Purim, this book is only the beginning of many happy, delicious, creative holiday celebrations in your home.

Chapter 1

SHABBAT

"And God blessed the seventh day and made it holy."

Genesis 2:3

I n every culture and every religion one day a week is set aside as a day to rest from the labors of the week and to prepare mentally, physically, and spiritually for the week to come. In Judaism, this is a sacred and holy day—more holy, in fact, than any other holiday or festival on the Jewish calendar. For on Shabbat, Hebrew for the Sabbath, Jews are called on to renew their faith in God, who proclaimed: "Remember the seventh day and keep it holy" (Exodus 20:8).

Six days a week we try to dominate the world. We labor, mentally and physically, to make our lives better.

Every day is spent in an effort to improve our standard of living or increase our knowledge. As the week progresses, the pace becomes more and more frenetic—and then comes Shabbat, a day of introspection, a day on which you are to rest as if all of your work has been completed, rest even from the thought of labor.

WHY SHABBAT?

In the Sabbath afternoon prayer it is written: "May the children realize and understand that their rest comes from Thee, and that to rest means to sanctify Thy name." Thus, observing the laws of the Sabbath shows a respect for, and a love of, God. The Sabbath revolves around three things—joy, holiness, and rest—and every Sabbath custom reflects this.

What kinds of labors are not permitted on the Sabbath? According to the ancient rabbis who interpreted the word of God in a book called the *Talmud*, man was not to perform any tasks that were necessary for the construction and furnishing of the sanctuary in the desert. Today, the forbidden acts are interpreted to mean those that interfere with the physical world. This includes the handling of money, a symbol of the Israelites' idolization of the golden calf while Moses was on Mount Sinai receiving the Ten Commandments.

Also forbidden was the reaping of any crop. Today, this has been interpreted as a prohibition against the severing of a naturally growing plant from the place it is growing. Picking flowers, breaking tree branches, and cutting the grass are all forbidden on the Sabbath. Thus, Shabbat is a time to reaffirm the union between man and nature and man and man. In all, the rabbis declared thirty-nine forbidden acts (see page 15).

THE ARTISTIC TRADITION

Shabbat customs offered artists and craftspeople an opportunity to create beautiful candlesticks, wine glasses, and *challah* covers especially for use on this holiday. Candlesticks hundreds of years old have been found, as have

Opposite page: These Russian candlesticks, made of cast and pounded silver, date from 1850. Above: This woodcut portrays a Shabbat evening meal. Note that the candles are the sole source of illumination in the room.

wine cups and spice boxes made from silver, gold, brass, glass, and ivory, carefully engraved and sometimes inlaid with precious and semiprecious stones. Woodcuts depicting the lighting of the Sabbath candles have also been preserved, serving not only as decoration, but also as proof that these same customs have been carried on for hundreds of years.

PREPARING FOR THE SABBATH

Special preparations are made before welcoming the Sabbath. The house is cleaned and the food is cooked beforehand, as the "kindling of a fire" is a forbidden act. It is customary to wear good or new clothing on Shabbat. Spiritual preparations are also important, as the mind needs to be completely empty of all "weekday" thoughts. Traditionally, it was customary to immerse oneself in the *mikveh*, the ritual bath, on Friday afternoon—to cleanse both the body and the soul.

OBSERVING THE SABBATH

The traditional Shabbat ceremony has been handed down for thousands of years. Following is a traditional celebration.

The Shabbat Candles

The first act of observance on the Sabbath is the lighting of the candles, signifying harmony in the home and Sabbath joy.

The Shabbat candles are traditionally lit by a woman in the room where the evening meal will be eaten. If no woman is present, a man may light the candles. The candles can be lit up to an hour and fifteen minutes before sundown, but the ideal time is fewer than eighteen minutes before. At least two candles should be lit—one to "remember" and the other to "observe" the Sabbath—but it is permissible by Jewish law to light more. Many families choose to light two candles plus an additional one for each child.

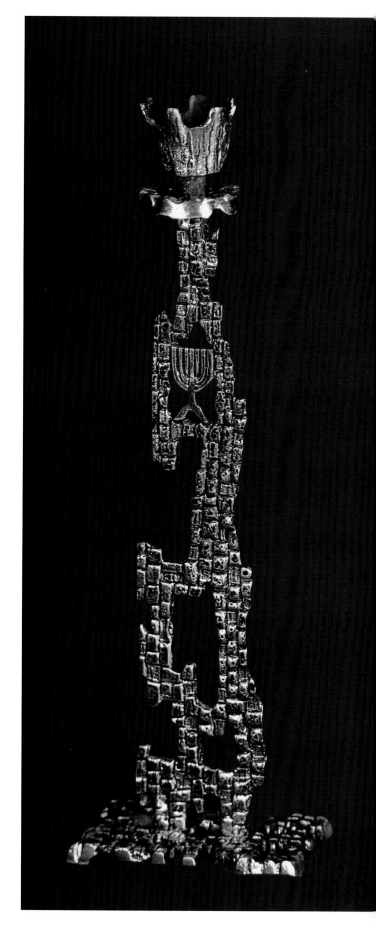

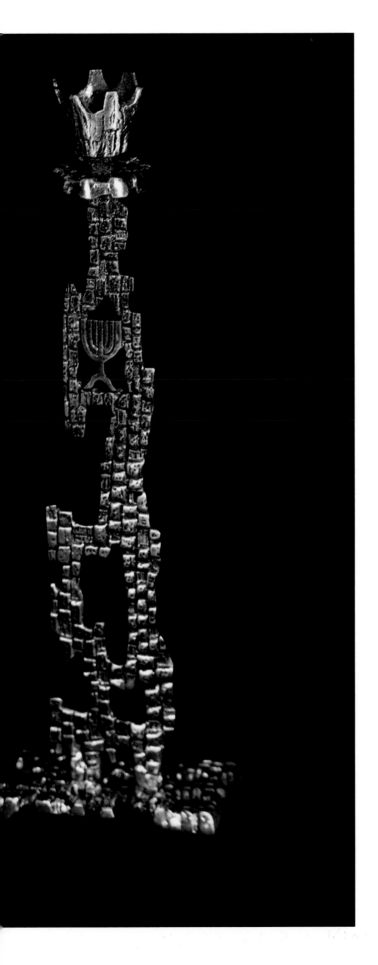

Blessing for Lighting the Candles

Blessed are You, Lord our God, King of the Universe, who has sanctified us with His commandments and commanded us to light the Shabbat candles.

Shabbat candlesticks provide craftspeople with a way to beautify and personalize the Sabbath observance.

Kiddush cups range from simple engraved silver to etched and stamped silver and gold. The silver cup on the right was created in Russia, sometime in the middle of the nineteenth century.

The candle-lighting ritual is a beautiful tradition—one that is handed down from mother to daughter, from generation to generation. The order of the ritual is as follows: The hands are drawn around the candles seven times. This symbolizes the culmination of six days of creation, leading to the seventh day of rest, and also draws warmth and light unto oneself. Next, the eyes are covered by the hands and the blessing is recited.

All efforts to use the light from the candles should be made, otherwise the blessing is wasted and invalidated. If no candles are available, a gas or electric light can be used instead (but it must be lit *before* sundown).

Kabbalat Shabbat

Once the candles have been lit, the *Kabbalat Shabbat* (Welcoming the Sabbath) service begins with the blessing of the children by the father. He places his lips on the forehead of each child and says: "May God make you like

Ephraim and Menasheh" or "May God make you like Sarah, Rebekah, Rachel, and Leah."

Next, "*Shalom Aleichem*" ("Peace Be unto You") is sung as a welcoming and as an offer of hospitality to the angels who accompany us during Shabbat. After this, the husband sings the "Woman of Valor" to his wife, extolling her virtues and declaring his love and appreciation for her. There was a time when this custom had fallen into disuse, but it has again become an important part of the Shabbat celebration.

Next come two prayers: One is called the *kiddush* and is said over a brimming cup of wine—a symbol of overflowing joy and bounty—and the second is said over the challah, which is cut and distributed to each person at the table. *Shabbat shalom*—a good and peaceful Shabbat—is wished to everyone present. After this, a large meal, the first of three to be eaten on Shabbat, is consumed. The rest of the night is spent talking to family and friends or studying the *Torah*.

Shabbat Morning

While the theme of Shabbat evening is harmony and joy, the theme for the next day is revelation. The Torah is read and often discussed in the synagogue. After morning services, but before the next meal, the kiddush is again recited, usually over wine, but another beverage may be used since it may be a little early in the day for wine. The challah is blessed and the meal is served.

Usually, meat is eaten at the afternoon meal, although more and more people are choosing to substitute a light dairy meal instead. This meal is both joyous and revealing—songs are sung and Torah is taught. After the meal is a time for relaxation. The form this takes differs for everyone: Some people take a short nap, others like to take a walk or visit with friends. In any case, as the day wears on, an effort to learn Torah should be made.

This beautifully embroidered velvet case holds tefillin and a prayer book for Shabbat services.

Havdalah

Another beautiful Shabbat custom is the *Havdalah* service, which symbolizes both the end of Shabbat and the coming together of its two themes.

The ceremony occurs forty-two minutes after dark, after the third meal is eaten. It consists of a candle made up of at least two separate wicks, usually six to eight inches long; a large, full cup of wine or another beverage, signifying bounty and joy; and a spice box filled with cloves or other fragrant spices or flowers. To properly celebrate Havdalah, all lights, with the exception of the havdalah candle, should be extinguished.

The candle, symbolizing the divine in man, is lit before the ceremony begins and given to a young child to hold. Next, the wine is blessed, but not drunk. Then, the spices, symbolic of the spiritual riches of Shabbat, are blessed and passed around for all to smell so as to dispel sadness over the end of Shabbat. Next, the candle is blessed by spreading the hands toward the candlelight so that the light from it is reflected in the fingernails with the shadow projected onto the palms of the hands. This symbolizes both the receiving of the light and the division between light and dark. Finally, the person reciting Havdalah drinks the cup of wine—saving a few drops to be poured into a dish to extinguish the candle—or passes it around for all present to sip. The ceremony ends with everyone wishing *shavuah tov* (a good week), and singing "*Eliahu ha-Navi*."

> ### Eliahu ha-Navi
>
> Elijah the prophet, Elijah the Tishbite, Elijah the Gilead, may he soon come to us with the Messiah son of David.

This silver filigreed spice box was made in Vienna. The filigree enables the scent to permeate the room.

MENU: FRIDAY NIGHT SUPPER

Alphabet Chicken Soup

Beef Brisket with Potatoes and Carrots

Buckwheat Groats (Kasha) and Bow Ties

Tossed Green Salad

Challah

Fresh Fruit

Alphabet Chicken Soup

1 chicken (4½ pounds), quartered	½ cup chopped carrot
2 pounds chicken wings	½ cup chopped parsley
4 quarts water	1 carrot, sliced
1 large onion, chopped	black pepper
½ cup chopped celery	½ cup alphabet noodles

Place the chicken, chicken wings, and water in a 10-quart pot. Bring the water to a boil, then turn the heat to simmer. Any white foam that forms can be removed with a spoon and discarded. Add the chopped onion, celery, and carrot to the pot. Cover the pot and continue to cook for ½ hour. Remove the quartered chicken from the pot and set aside.

Continue cooking the remaining chicken wings and vegetables for another 30 minutes. Strain the soup, keeping the broth. If you wish to use the chicken from the wings, save them and allow to cool. Otherwise, discard both the chicken wings and the remaining vegetables.

To the broth, add the parsley, sliced carrot, black pepper, and alphabet noodles, cover, and cook for another 20 minutes.

Meanwhile, remove the chicken from the wings, cut into small pieces, and put back into the soup.

The chicken from the chicken parts should be skinned, removed from the bone, and cut into chunks. This chicken should be refrigerated and used for chicken salad for the Saturday meal.

Yield: 16 servings

Beef Brisket with Potatoes and Carrots

2 onions, sliced	4- to 5-pound beef brisket
5 carrots, sliced	8-ounce can tomato sauce
1 stalk celery, sliced	5 baking potatoes,
2 bay leaves	peeled and quartered

In the bottom of a Dutch oven with a lid, place the onions, carrots, celery, and bay leaves. Add the meat to the pot.

Pour the tomato sauce over the meat. Fill the empty sauce can with water and then pour that over the meat.

Bring the pot to a boil over high heat, cover the pan, and then allow it to cook on low heat for about 1½ hours. Add the quartered potatoes and continue cooking for 30 minutes or until meat and potatoes are tender.

Remove the meat from the pot and place it on a large plate to allow it to cool slightly before cutting. Slice the meat and serve with the gravy on the side. The vegetables can be served separately or as part of the gravy.

The brisket can be made one day and served the next; the fat will have cooled and can easily be removed and discarded.

Yield: 10 to 12 servings

Buckwheat groats and bow ties.

Buckwheat Groats (Kasha) and Bow Ties

1 tablespoon olive oil
½ cup chopped onion
1 egg, beaten
1 cup whole or medium buckwheat groats
2 cups boiling water
2 cups egg bow-tie noodles

Heat the oil in a medium saucepan. Add the onions and sauté on low heat until they are softened.

With a fork, combine the egg and buckwheat groats in a bowl. Add to the onion in the saucepan and stir and mix until the buckwheat kernels are separated and somewhat dry.

Now add the boiling water to the buckwheat. Mix well, cover, and allow to cook for 10 minutes.

Meanwhile, cook the noodles. When the noodles are cooked, combine with the cooked buckwheat and serve with the brisket gravy.

Yield: 6 cups

Tossed Green Salad

8 red-leaf lettuce leaves or romaine leaves
1 carrot, shredded
8 black olives
¼ cup chopped onion
1 half-cucumber, thinly sliced
½ cup shredded red cabbage

Tear lettuce leaves and combine with remaining ingredients in a large salad bowl. Toss with Mustard Vinaigrette Dressing before serving.

Yield: 8 servings

Mustard Vinaigrette Dressing

½ cup red wine vinegar   1 tablespoon coarse mustard
¼ cup olive oil   1 teaspoon chopped fresh basil

Combine ingredients and beat with a wire whisk. Add enough to salad to moisten and flavor and then toss.

Yield: ¾ cup

Challah

2 ounces compressed yeast or 2 packages dry yeast
1¼ cups lukewarm water
¼ cup sugar
⅓ cup vegetable oil
1 teaspoon salt
3 eggs, beaten
5 to 6¼ cups unbleached flour
1 egg
1 tablespoon honey
poppy seeds, optional
½ cup raisins, optional (see note)

In a large mixing bowl, dissolve the yeast in the lukewarm water, mixing with a spoon to combine. Add the sugar, oil, salt, and the 3 beaten eggs, mixing well. Add 4 cups of the flour, gradually beating into the mixture. The batter will be lumpy and runny.

Add more flour, using the spoon to combine, until the dough is too thick to beat. The dough should be stiff but sticky.

Turn the dough out onto a floured board. With floured hands, knead the dough for 5 to 10 minutes, adding flour as necessary to make a smooth and stretchy dough.

Place the dough in an oiled bowl, turning once to coat the dough with oil. Cover the bowl with a cloth and allow the dough to rise in a warm place until it doubles in bulk. This will take about 1 hour.

Punch dough down and divide the dough into 2 parts. Divide each part into 3 equal pieces. Roll these pieces into strips about 12 inches long. Pinch 3 strips together at the top and then braid them together. Place this into an oiled 9 × 5-inch loaf pan (during Rosh Hashanah the challah is baked in a round pan). Repeat with the other 3 strips. Cover the 2 loaves and let rise for ½ hour or until the dough rises to the top of the pan.

Combine the egg and the honey and brush this mixture over the loaves. Sprinkle with poppy seeds. Bake at 375 degrees F for 30 minutes. Cool for 20 minutes and remove from the pans.

Yield: 2 loaves

Note: Raisin Challah: After the dough has been kneaded for 5 to 10 minutes, knead the ½ cup raisins into the dough. Rather than baking the bread in bread pans, the loaves can be placed on oiled baking sheets or the dough can be shaped into 2 round loaves and placed on the baking sheets to rise.

MENU: SATURDAY COLD MEAL

Chunky Chicken Salad

**Romaine, Chickpea, Shredded Carrot,
Mushroom, and Olive Salad**

Mom's Best Potato Salad

Fresh Melon Wedge

Hard Rolls

Chunky Chicken Salad

4 cups cooked chicken, cut into chunks
¼ cup chopped celery
¼ cup finely sliced green onions
1 tablespoon chopped fresh dill
⅓ cup light mayonnaise
romaine lettuce leaves

Combine all the ingredients except romaine leaves. Refrigerate until serving time. Serve on the bed of greens.

Yield: 4 servings

Romaine, Chickpea, Shredded Carrot, Mushroom, and Olive Salad

8 romaine leaves
1 cup cooked chickpeas
1 carrot, shredded
8 mushrooms, sliced
8 ripe olives, sliced

Wash, drain, and tear romaine leaves into bite-size pieces and put in salad bowl. Add remaining ingredients. Pour Apple Vinaigrette Dressing over the salad in bowl, toss, and serve immediately or toss with salad dressing before serving.

Yield: 4 servings

Apple Vinaigrette Dressing

2 tablespoons olive oil
2 tablespoons frozen apple juice concentrate
¼ cup red wine vinegar

Using a wire whisk, beat the olive oil, apple juice concentrate, and wine vinegar together in a small bowl.

Yield: ½ cup

Mom's Best Potato Salad

3 large Idaho potatoes
2 teaspoons sugar
2 teaspoons apple cider vinegar
½ cup chopped onion
½ cup chopped celery
¼ cup chopped parsley
1 teaspoon celery seed
¾ cup light mayonnaise

Wash potatoes, cut into large chunks, and place in saucepan. Cover with water. Bring to a boil and cook until potatoes are tender, about 20 minutes. Drain potatoes and peel.

Cut potatoes into bite-size chunks and place in serving bowl. Sprinkle sugar and vinegar over potatoes. Add onion, celery, parsley, and celery seed. Finally, add light mayonnaise and mix all ingredients thoroughly. Serve immediately or cover and refrigerate until serving time.

Yield: 6 servings

CRAFTS

Shabbat Candles

Shabbat is begun with the lighting of two candles, perhaps the most commonly practiced ritual among Jews. It is a tradition that bonds Jews with each other around the world and has been a strong element in keeping Jewish culture alive.

Materials Needed:

> paraffin wax (approximately 2 pounds)
> double boiler
> colored crayons
> mixing spoon or stick
> wicks, approximately 12 inches each (1 per candle)

Coloring the Wax:

Over a low flame, melt some paraffin, a little bit at a time, in a double boiler (the inner pot should be a can or something else you don't mind melting wax in). Make sure the melted wax is at least 8 inches deep. Add colored crayons (without wrappers) and mix gently until you've achieved the color desired.

Dipping the Candles:

Firmly hold one end of a wick, and dip carefully into the melted wax and pull out. Allow the wax to harden on the wick and dip it again. Continue the dipping and hardening process until the candle is about 1 inch thick. Make sure not to keep the wick in the wax too long or the heated wax will melt off previous layers.

Multicolored Candles:

For different colored layers, create several colors of melted wax and alternate colors when dipping the wicks.

Shabbat Candlesticks

Materials Needed:

> salt (enough to fill both spice bottles)
> colored chalk
> 2 small empty spice bottles with lids
> pencil
> glue
> 2 soda-bottle caps
> aluminum foil
> black paint
> paint brush
> candles

The Colors:

Pour some salt onto a piece of newspaper or scrap paper. Roll sticks of chalk in the salt, one at a time, until it becomes a color you'd like to use. Make several piles of colored salt of varying amounts, making certain that there is enough salt to fill both bottles.

The Pattern:

Pour an equal amount of one color of salt in both bottles. Then pour an equal amount of another color in both bottles. Insert a pencil into a bottle and gently push down the bottom color at one point by drawing an imaginary line downward on the side of the jar. Continue this pattern by pushing down the bottom color every ¼ inch or so. Pour a third layer of color in each bottle and then push down the second color in between the indents of the first layer. Fill both jars by alternating colored layers and creating the wave pattern with a pencil. Light a candle and drip enough wax into each jar to seal the salt in.

The Tops:

Glue the soda-bottle caps, upside down, to the tops of the spice bottle lids. Allow the glue to harden and then carefully cover lids and caps with aluminum foil. For a tarnished look, paint each black, and, after they dry, rub off some of the paint. Screw each lid onto the filled spice jar. To use the candlesticks, let candle wax drip into the bottle cap and set the candles in the heated wax.

Challah Cover

One of the many ways Shabbat is distinguished from other days of the week is by eating special bread, or challah. Some Jews say that they cover the challah so it won't be "insulted" that the wine is blessed before it is during the Kabbalat Shabbat. Others believe the challah symbolizes the manna which fell from the heavens to feed the Israelites as they wandered in the wilderness after their Exodus from Egypt, and they use a challah cover to represent the dew which covered the manna eaten by their ancestors. Still others see the use of a challah cover in purely practical terms: It keeps the bread fresh and warm!

Materials Needed:

fabric crayon	**iron**
needle	**embroidery floss**
20 × 16-inch piece of linen cloth	

Adhering the Pattern:

Photocopy the pattern shown here and "trace" it with stitching marks onto paper with fabric crayon. Place the design in position, face down on the fabric. Now, transfer the pattern onto the fabric with a cool iron.

Cross-Stitching:

Following the pattern exactly, embroider the design using 3 threads from a skein of floss. Cross-stitch and chain-stitch will work best. Hem the edges of the cloth if it is unfinished.

The design becomes more personal by the colors you choose to embroider with.

Spice Box

Shabbat ends at sunset with Havdalah. During the ceremony, samim, or spices, are passed around so all can share their aroma.

Materials Needed:

hammer and nail	**varied buttons**
small jar with lid	**1 tablespoon cloves**
rubber cement	**(enough to fill the jar)**
colored ribbon	

The Top:

Using a hammer and nail, punch a lot of holes in the jar's lid. Next, with rubber cement, glue colored ribbon to the edge of the lid. Now, glue the buttons to the top. If buttons aren't available, dried beans of different colors and sizes are an excellent replacement.

The Scent:

When the rubber cement has dried, put cloves in the jar and screw the lid on tightly. You may have to wait a few days for the cement's odor to dissipate and the cloves' aroma to become more apparent.

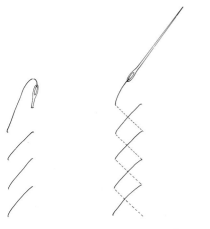

cross-stitch

chain-stitch

Chapter 2

ROSH HASHANAH: THE NEW YEAR

"In the seventh month, in the first day of the month, shall be a solemn rest unto you, a memorial proclaimed with the blast of horns, a holy convocation. Ye shall do no manner of servile work; and ye shall bring an offering made by fire unto the Lord."

Leviticus 23: 23–25

Above: This etching depicts the reading of the Torah. Rosh Hashanah, literally the "The Head of the Year," is the time when the Torah scrolls are rerolled so that they can be read from the beginning. Opposite page: These wooden yadim, more commonly known as pointers, come from a synagogue in Prague. Usually made in the form of a hand, they are used for reading the Torah.

osh Hashanah, literally "The Head of the Year," is the culmination of a month-long period of study and self-examination. It is a day of judgment, a day of joy, and a time of renewal. As a day of judgment, Rosh Hashanah, also called *Yom ha-Din*, is a solemn time, a time to confront the deeds of the past year and reconcile with oneself and with anyone whom one has hurt or wronged. As a day of joy, Rosh Hashanah commemorates the birth of the world, the wondrous act of creation. And as a time of renewal, Rosh Hashanah offers Jews an opportunity to reaffirm their faith in God and to contemplate His faith in His people.

THE ORIGINS OF ROSH HASHANAH

Rosh Hashanah falls on the first day of the Jewish month of *Tishri*. One explanation of its origin says that on this day, the patriarch Abraham offered Isaac to God as proof of his devotion. Abraham's willingness to sacrifice the son he adored was a profound act aimed at proving his faithfulness to God. As is well known, Abraham was permitted to sacrifice a lamb instead, and God's faith in man was renewed.

It is also believed that the prophet Samuel was born on this day. Hannah, a childless Jewish woman, promised God the absolute devotion of her child should He be so

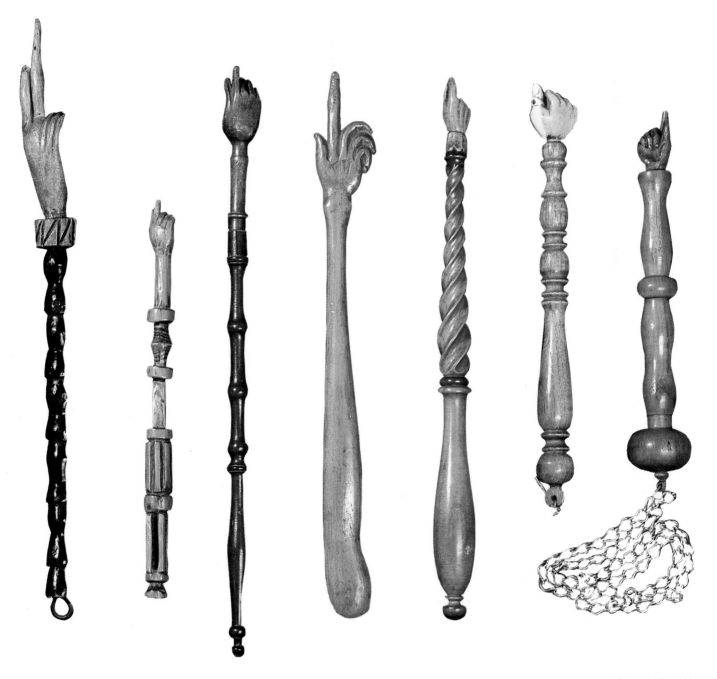

compassionate as to grant her a son. God did so, and the prophet Samuel was born.

It is interesting to note that while the Bible states that the first day of Tishri is to be set aside as a holiday, there is no specific reference to this day as Rosh Hashanah. It is believed that during biblical times no holiday of this name was ever celebrated. In fact, before the destruction of the second temple and the Babylonian exile in 70 C.E., only one holiday was observed at this time of the year, the Festival of Ingathering of Fruits and Grapes. Today, this festival has been divided into three separate holidays: Rosh Hashanah, Yom Kippur, and Sukkot.

PREPARING FOR ROSH HASHANAH

Emotional and spiritual preparations for Rosh Hashanah begin during the month of *Elul*, which precedes the month of Tishri. Elul is intended as a time for study and self-examination, and a time to review the past year and prepare for repentance.

Many traditions are associated with the month of Elul. The first is the blowing of the *shofar*, the horn of a ram, every morning except on Shabbat and on the last day of the month. The blast of the shofar is intended as a sort of spiritual alarm, reminding people to begin their soul-searching. It is also a prelude to the more extensive shofar-blowing that is a fundamental part of the Rosh

Above: One of the central features of the Rosh Hashanah service is the blowing of the shofar. Opposite page: This red velvet ark cover is used only on the high holidays. Made in Danzig in 1795, it is velvet with metallic lace, silk embroidery, metallic foil, and glass stone.

Hashanah service. (The shofar is not blown on Shabbat because it was once feared that the desire to blow the shofar would become all-consuming, and also that the prohibition against carrying an object from a public place to a private one would be forgotten or ignored in the desire to hear the wonderful, mysterious sound it makes.)

It is also customary to read Psalm 27 during prayer services in the month of Elul: "The Lord is my light and my salvation; whom shall I fear? The Lord is the stronghold of my life; of whom shall I be afraid? When evildoers came upon me to eat up my flesh, even mine adversaries and my foes, they stumbled and fell." This is invoked as a plea to God to help us when tormented by our enemies, as a way of showing us that He still believes in our faith in Him.

Another custom observed during this month, usually the day before Rosh Hashanah, is visiting the graves of family, friends, and teachers to remember the sanctity of their lives and to gain inspiration for the coming year. Remembering and facing death is symbolic of acknowledging the death of the old self, making room for the birth of a new self. It is from this custom that Rosh Hashanah has gained another name, *Yom ha-Zikkaron*, or the "Day of Memorial."

Giving *tzedekah*, or charity, during Elul is another custom and is considered a *mitzvah*, or good deed.

ROSH HASHANAH

35

Slichot

As Elul draws to a close, final preparations are made to usher in the new year. The period beginning on the Sunday before the start of Rosh Hashanah is known as *slichot*, or "forgiveness." During slichot, special prayers invoking the grace of God are recited at the morning service. These prayers remind us of God's past acts of love and kindness in response to our entreaties. This is an intense period, and is also the proper time to express or show remorse for the hurt we have caused God and others and to ask forgiveness.

These old Rosh Hashanah cards show both the solemnity of the holiday as well as the joy involved in welcoming the new year.

OBSERVING ROSH HASHANAH

As the sun sets on the first day of Tishri, families and friends gather in their homes to light the candles, officially welcoming the new year. Once this act is complete, the kiddush—the blessing over the wine—and the *hamotzi*—the blessing over the bread—are recited. Next, it is customary to dip an apple in honey and say: "Blessed are you, Lord our God, King of the Universe, who creates the fruit of the tree." After the apple and honey are eaten, the prayer continues: "May it be Your will, God and God of our fathers, to renew on us a good and sweet year." On this night a big meal is prepared, and the challot (plural for challah) are baked in a circular shape, symbolizing the cycle of the year.

All food prepared and eaten on Rosh Hashanah should be sweet, for the hope of a sweet year; round, for the cycle of the year; and abundant, for fruitfulness and prosperity in the year to come. On the second night of the new year it is traditional to eat a new fruit, one that you have not yet eaten that season.

The Shofar

The essential feature of the Rosh Hashanah-day service is the blowing of the shofar. (If Rosh Hashanah falls on the Sabbath, the blowing of the shofar is omitted [see page 34].) Its use is thought to recall an earlier time of primitive cultures, when people would make noise and create pandemonium to drive away evil spirits.

The shofar is usually the horn of a ram, but it can actually be any horn that comes from a kosher animal except a cow or a calf, which might serve to recall the disgrace caused to the Israelites by their worshipping of the golden calf while Moses was on Mount Sinai receiving the Ten Commandments. It may not be painted, but it can be adorned with carved or inscribed designs, most often beautiful scrollwork and sayings from the Bible.

The blowing of the shofar requires considerable talent, and people are specially trained for this purpose. The notes are prescribed by tradition, and no deviation from this order is permitted. The shofar can make three basic sounds: *teki'yah*, a short blast, a bass note that ends abruptly; *teru'ah*, a trump, a long resonant blast; and *shebarim*, a quaver, a series of trill blasts.

The shofar is blown during the morning service of Rosh Hashanah and is repeated four times during the service. The first time it is sounded to celebrate God's kingship. The second time it is sounded for remembrance. The third time it is intended to bring to mind all of the events, both in the past and in the future, that are linked with the blowing of the ram's horn. It is sounded a final time toward the end of the service, bringing the first three aspects together.

Tashlikh

On the afternoon of the first day of the new year, it is customary to perform a ritual known as *tashlikh*, which involves walking to a river or to any other body of water to recite special penitentiary prayers. Tashlikh is based on the following biblical passage: "You will cast all their sins into the depths of the sea, and may You cast all the sins of Your people, the house of Israel, into a place where they shall be no more remembered or visited or ever come to mind." The prayer is accompanied by either the emptying of one's pockets into the water or casting bread crumbs into the water, symbolizing the casting-off of our sins, which are carried off by the running water, and the beginning of the new year.

L'shanah Tovah

A final Rosh Hashanah custom is to send friends and family cards with the saying: *L'shanah tovah*, "to a good and healthy year." (For instructions on making your own Rosh Hashanah cards, see page 41.)

MENU: ROSH HASHANAH EVE SUPPER

Savory Baked Chicken

Oven Browned Potatoes with Garlic

Marinated Pepper Salad on Fresh Greens

Snap Beans with Mushrooms and Pine Nuts

Round Challah (see page 23)

Nut and Honey Cake

Savory Baked Chicken

> 3-pound broiler/fryer chicken, cut into 8 pieces
> 2 egg whites
> ¾ cup oat bran
> 1 teaspoon garlic powder
> 1 teaspoon onion powder
> 1 teaspoon paprika
> 1 teaspoon basil leaves
> 1 teaspoon dry mustard
> ½ teaspoon black pepper

Remove skin from chicken. Put egg whites in a pie pan and beat slightly. Combine remaining ingredients in another pie pan. Dip chicken into egg whites and then into dry ingredients, turning to coat. If coating looks dry, moisten with any remaining egg white.

Place coated chicken pieces into a baking pan and bake at 350 degrees F for 60 minutes.

Yield: 8 servings

Oven Browned Potatoes with Garlic

> 4 to 6 medium red-skinned potatoes
> 2 tablespoons olive oil
> 1 garlic clove, minced

Wash and peel potatoes and cut into quarters. Spread the oil in an 8 × 8-inch pan. Add the garlic and spread evenly over the bottom of the pan. Place the potatoes over the garlic and oil. Bake at 350 degrees F for 1 hour, turning occasionally to brown on all sides.

Yield: 4 to 6 servings

Marinated Pepper Salad on Fresh Greens

> 1 sweet red pepper
> 1 sweet yellow pepper
> 2 tablespoons olive oil
> ¼ cup red wine vinegar
> 1 clove garlic, minced
> 8 romaine leaves
> 4 slices red onion
> 8 large black olives

First, the sweet peppers must be roasted. To do this, wash the peppers and place them on a broiling pan. Broil in the oven for 20 minutes, turning them every 5 minutes so that each side can be broiled until blackened. When all sides are blackened, remove the peppers from the oven and place them in a small brown bag. Keep the peppers in the bag until they have cooled, about 30 minutes. Remove the blackened skin from the peppers, then core and seed them. Slice the peppers into thin strips, about ¼ × 2 inches long.

Place the olive oil, vinegar, and garlic in a small bowl or refrigerator-storage container. Add the roasted pepper slices to this and refrigerate, covered, until chilled or overnight.

When ready to prepare and serve salad, wash romaine and place in individual salad bowls or on plates. Place some of the roasted pepper on the romaine. Garnish with the sliced red onion and the black olives. Spoon some of the marinade over the salad.

Yield: 4 servings

Nut and honey cake.

Snap Beans with Mushrooms and Pine Nuts

1 pound snap beans	2 teaspoons olive oil
2 tablespoons pine nuts	1 cup sliced mushrooms

Wash and cut ends off beans. Bring about an inch of water to a boil in a 2-quart saucepan. Add the beans and cook, covered, for 8 to 10 minutes or until tenderness preferred.

While beans are cooking, toast pine nuts in a small, dry skillet over medium-high heat. Toast until golden, being careful not to burn. Remove pine nuts and set aside.

In same skillet, add olive oil and then mushrooms. Sauté mushrooms until softened.

When beans are cooked, drain and pour them into a serving bowl. Add the toasted pine nuts and sautéed mushrooms. Toss and serve.

Yield: 6 servings

Nut and Honey Cake

4 cups unbleached flour	½ cup sugar
2 teaspoons baking powder	1 cup honey
¼ teaspoon baking soda	4 tablespoons oil
1 teaspoon cinnamon	1 cup strong cold coffee
½ teaspoon ground cloves	1 cup slivered almonds
3 eggs	

Combine the flour, baking powder, baking soda, cinnamon, and ground cloves in a bowl.

In another bowl, beat the eggs. Add the sugar and honey and beat together. Add the oil. Now add some of the dry ingredients and some of the cold coffee and mix well. Add the remaining dry ingredients and the remaining coffee. Add the nuts.

Pour the batter into 2 well-greased 9 × 5-inch bread pans. Bake for 45 minutes at 350 degrees F.

Yield: 2 cakes

CRAFTS

Rosh Hashanah Cards

Materials Needed:

soft pencil
index card
X-Acto knife
sponge cut into 2-inch pieces
several colors of tempera paint
colored paper

Making the Stencils:

Trace the patterns (see figures 1, 2, and 3) with a soft pencil and place them face down on the index card. Rub the other side of the patterns with the pencil and remove them; there should be a mirror image of the patterns on the cardboard. Cut the patterns from the cardboard using the X-Acto knife. Save the cut-out portion of figure 1.

Printing the Patterns:

Lightly dip a piece of sponge into one color of paint. Place the cut-out portion of figure 1 on the colored paper where you'd like the design to appear and paint around it using the sponge. Fill in a portion or all of the other stencils with whatever colors you choose using separate pieces of sponge for each color. Repeat as many times as you like, repositioning the stencil each time and allowing it to dry between the use of different colors.

Finishing the Card:

Fold the colored paper in half, painted-side out. If you've chosen a dark color, glue a lighter sheet of paper inside for writing on.

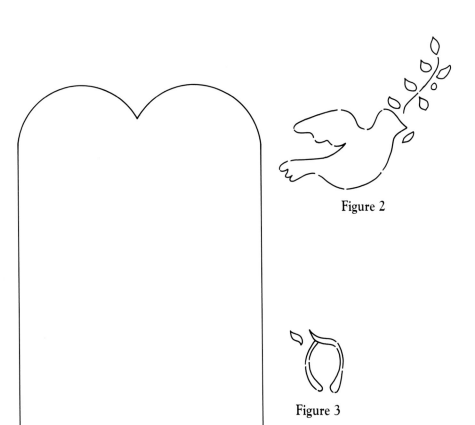

Figure 2

Figure 3

Figure 1

Rosh Hashanah card.

Chapter 3

YOM KIPPUR:
THE DAY OF ATONEMENT

"For on this day shall atonement be made for you, to cleanse you; from all your sins shall ye be clean before the Lord. It is a sabbath of solemn rest unto you, and ye shall afflict your souls; it is a statute for ever."

Leviticus 16:30–31

This French woodcut depicts the celebration of Yom Kippur, a day of self-denial that is spent in the synagogue.

Yom Kippur, which falls on the tenth day of Tishri, is the holiest day of the Jewish year. It is a day of transcendent joy, a day of restoration, and a day of self-denial. Its ultimate intention is to cleanse the soul of sin before God. As such, it provides a yearly opportunity to obtain divine forgiveness through penitence and prayer. On this day, the Jew feels the strongest sense of partnership with God, knowing that if he struggles to redress the wrongs he has committed, God will offer forgiveness.

THE DAYS OF AWE

The ten days between Rosh Hashanah and Yom Kippur are known as the "Days of Awe," and they are dedicated to the cleansing of the soul, both physically and spiritually. It is customary to fast until noon on each of these ten days, except on the Sabbath and on the day preceding Yom Kippur, and to abstain from all physical pleasures and entertainment as well. It is also a time of self-scrutiny and introspection, during which one asks forgiveness for the past year's transgressions. It is a difficult yet ultimately hopeful period, for the soul is both agitated and healed by such ruminations.

The ten Days of Awe are different from most other Jewish holy days in that they bear no relation to nature or to any historical event in the past. Instead, they are concerned only with religious feelings and inner probings. This religious dedication is displayed in the recitation of special prayers of penitence and supplicatory psalms every morning at dawn. At the end of these ten days, Yom Kippur begins.

This wool tallis (prayer shawl) is typical of those worn in synagogue on the high holidays.

This etching shows the interior of a synagogue on Yom Kippur. Note the elaborately embroidered table covers, used only during the high holidays.

THE ORIGINS OF YOM KIPPUR

The ritual of Yom Kippur is thought to be based upon an ancient and special ceremony aimed at purging the defilements of the Shrine and the Israelites in general. In this ritual, the high priest brought a bull and two goats to the temple as sacrifices. First, the bull was sacrificed to purge the Shrine from the profanities of the priest and his household. Then one of the goats was chosen by lot to be sacrificed to purify the temple from any profanities caused by the Jews. Once this goat was chosen for sacrifice, the other goat was sent to wander in the wilderness, but only after the priest placed both hands on the goat's head and, in this symbolic gesture, laid there all of the sins of the people.

In the Bible, the earliest account of Yom Kippur is found in the sixteenth chapter of Leviticus, where it is said to have been initiated by Moses in connection with the tabernacle erected in the wilderness. This account seems to have been written centuries after the fact, and the ceremonies it describes are all based on primitive practices.

OBSERVING YOM KIPPUR

Yom Kippur is marked by a strict fast, observed for the sake of physical mortification and purgation of the soul. The fast includes abstention from food and water, washing the body, wearing cosmetics, perfumes, or leather shoes, and sexual intercourse; those who are sick or weak are exempt. In addition, all forms of work are to be discontinued from sunset the first night through sunset the following night.

Customs

An old, unusual custom called *kapparot*, now practiced only by Orthodox Jews the day before Yom Kippur, involves swinging a live chicken around one's head, saying: "This is my change, this is my compensation, this is my redemption. This cock is going to be killed, and I shall enter upon a long, happy, and peaceful life." This ritual is symbolic of doing penance for our sins. When the rite is completed, the chicken is slaughtered and given to the poor. Today, a more popular version of this custom exists in which the same prayer is recited while a money-filled handkerchief is swung around the head. Following this, the money is given to charity.

Other customs practiced on Yom Kippur include spending the evening and entire day in synagogue. It is customary for pious Jews to remove their shoes before entering the sanctuary, don felt slippers, and remain standing from the beginning to the end of the services. Many Jews spend the entire night in meditation or studying en-

tries in the Talmud that relate to the holiday. It is traditional to cloak the scrolls of the Torah in white mantles and to deck the ark with a white curtain, both symbols of purity. Throughout the day the ark is kept open, and the cantor is flanked by two assistants in case he falls sick or falters in his prayers.

Services

The focus of Yom Kippur is active participation in prayer services. In fact, five separate services are conducted during the twenty-four-hour period this holiday is observed. The devotions begin a few minutes before sunset, and it is hoped that even the most recalcitrant and unobservant Jews will return to the fold for this service. It is believed that this custom was started during the Spanish Inquisition, to permit those who had been forcibly converted to Christianity to clandestinely rejoin their brethren. At this time, all but one of the Torah scrolls are removed from the ark and carried in a procession to the rostrum.

They are then returned to the ark and the evening service begins.

Kol Nidre is the first of the five services conducted on Yom Kippur. It begins when the sun is still on the horizon and ends when the sun has set. Kol Nidre, translated as "All Vows," is comprised of special penitentiary prayers and by the alphabetical confession of sins (aggressed, betrayed, cheated . . .). These are followed by prayers for pardon. A unique aspect of these prayers is that they are recited in a collective sense—"*We* have trespassed . . ." These prayers are recited three times: first in a whisper, then louder, and finally in clear, ringing tones.

The morning service is comprised of two full Torah services. The first involves reading Leviticus 16, which describes the sacrifices performed by the high priest on Yom Kippur, and Isaiah 57, which conveys the admonitions to others who are in need. The second is the *Musaf* service, which reenacts the ceremony followed when the temple stood in Jerusalem.

Minchah is the fourth service of Yom Kippur. Leviticus 18 is read, cataloging the forbidden sexual relationships that defile the soul. The Book of Jonah is also read. This is an allegory of an individual soul struggling between the hunger for death and oblivion and the readiness of that soul to be reborn. This reading comes at a time when our own stomachs are growling from hunger, making Jonah's plight seem all the more urgent to us.

The final service of Yom Kippur is the *Neilah*, the closing of the gates. (The gates are "opened" on Rosh Hashanah, allowing us to expose our sins.) At the end of this service, the shofar is blown, signaling the final sealing of the heavenly gates. By this time, the penitent Jew should have received forgiveness; the gates of penitence will not open again until Rosh Hashanah the next year. The service concludes with the congregants intoning the age-old wish of all Jews in the Diaspora: *L'shana ha-ba-ah b'Yerushalayim*—"next year in Jerusalem."

Once the services have concluded, families go home to break the fast. This same night, the construction of the *sukkah* begins.

MENU: YOM KIPPUR EVE SUPPER

Chopped Liver Pâté

Bean, Barley, and Mushroom Soup

Skillet Chicken and Rice

Sliced Onion, Orange, and Spinach Salad

Dried Fruit Compote

Chopped Liver Pâté

1 12-ounce container commercially frozen chopped liver
  (see note)
4 large eggs, hard cooked
lettuce cups
onion slices

Allow the liver to thaw in the refrigerator. Add to food processor along with the peeled eggs. Process using a metal blade. Serve on lettuce cups garnished with thinly sliced onion rings. This can also be used as a spread on crackers or thinly sliced appetizer slices of rye or black bread.

Yield: 6 appetizer servings

Note: To prepare calf's chopped liver from the basic ingredients, purchase a pound of calf's liver or use 8 chicken livers. Sauté 1 medium sliced onion in 2 tablespoons of corn oil. When the onion is translucent, add the liver to the saucepan. Sauté for 10 minutes, or until the liver is cooked through, turning as necessary. (In order to obey the kosher laws, the liver would have to be broiled so the blood would run out.) Then allow the liver to cool and process the liver and the onion in the food processor. A meat or food chopper can also be used; a blender would not make a satisfactory product. Add the eggs and proceed with the above recipe.

Bean, Barley, and Mushroom Soup

1 pound dried lima beans
2 pounds flank steak (flanken)
4 quarts water
3 onions, sliced
1 pound fresh mushrooms, sliced
1 pound carrots, chopped
1 turnip, coarsely chopped
3 stalks celery, chopped
½ cup chopped fresh parsley
½ cup barley
1 10¾-ounce can pareve tomato soup
1 teaspoon salt
½ teaspoon pepper

Add the lima beans to a pot, cover them with water, and bring the water to a boil. Then turn off the heat, cover the pot, and allow the beans to soak for 1 hour.

Place the meat and 4 quarts of water in a 10-quart pot. Bring the water to a boil, turn down the heat to simmer, and let the meat cook for 1 hour.

Now add to the meat the onions, mushrooms, carrots, turnip, celery, parsley, barley, and the drained, soaked lima beans. Continue cooking until the meat is tender and the vegetables are soft, about 45 to 60 minutes. Remove the meat from the soup and cut it into small pieces and return them to the soup. Add the can of tomato soup and the salt and pepper. Serve.

This soup can be kept in the refrigerator for several days if divided into quart containers. It also freezes well.

Yield: 5 quarts

Skillet chicken and rice.

Skillet Chicken and Rice

1½-pound boned and skinned chicken breast
2 tablespoons olive oil
2 cups sliced mushrooms (about ½ pound)
3 green onions, sliced
1 clove garlic, minced
½ cup dry white wine
1 teaspoon lemon juice
2½ cups water
1 cup white rice
10 green olives stuffed with pimientos, sliced in half

Cut chicken into large bite-size chunks. Heat olive oil in a large saucepan or skillet. Add mushrooms, onions, and garlic and sauté until the mushrooms are softened. Add the white wine and lemon juice. Add the chicken and, with the heat on medium, cover and allow the chicken to simmer for 10 minutes.

In a separate pot, bring the 2½ cups of water to a boil. Add the rice, cover, and turn down the heat to low. Cook for 15 minutes.

Remove the lid from the chicken and add the olives after the rice has been cooking 10 minutes. Continue to cook until all is heated through.

Place the rice on a serving platter. Pour the chicken mixture over the rice and serve.

Yield: 4 servings

Sliced Onion, Orange, and Spinach Salad

5 ounces fresh spinach
1 navel orange
2 slices red onion or
  any mild onion

2 tablespoons frozen apple
  juice concentrate
2 tablespoons red wine vinegar
1 tablespoon olive oil

Rinse spinach thoroughly and pat dry. Divide leaves among 4 salad plates.

Peel orange and slice in rounds, placing 2 slices of orange on each of the salads. Place 2 to 3 rings of the onion slices on top of the orange slices.

Combine the apple juice concentrate, red wine vinegar, and olive oil and whisk together. Divide this dressing among the 4 salads. Serve.

Yield: 4 servings

Sliced onion, orange, and spinach salad.

Dried Fruit Compote

8 ounces dried apricots
8 ounces dried prunes
1 apple, cored, quartered, and peeled
1 cup apple juice
1 cup water
2 tablespoons lemon juice

Add the ingredients to a saucepan. Bring the liquid to a boil, turn down the heat, and simmer for 15 minutes.

Yield: 8 servings

MENU: BREAKING THE FAST

Gefilte Fish

Creamed Cucumber Slices

Red Beets with Dill

Julienned Raw Vegetables

Yogurt Cheese Dip

Mandel Bread

Gefilte Fish

In the past, preparation of gefilte fish was an all-day project. It meant going to the fish market and finding the proper combination of fish, bringing it home, boning it, grinding it with vegetables, adding matzah meal and egg, and forming the mixture into balls. The balls were placed on top of the fish heads and bones and then cooked in water for several hours. Today, most families purchase gefilte fish in jars. Here is a recipe for gefilte fish that takes little time, since it is made with fillets that have been poached. Leftover cooked fish would also be good for this recipe.

3 cups water
1 pound raw white fish (haddock, pike)
2 carrots
1 stalk celery
2 small onions
1 egg
2 tablespoons matzah meal
1 teaspoon sugar
salt and pepper to taste
lettuce leaves
beet horseradish

In a shallow pan, bring the 3 cups of water to a boil. Add fish and simmer for 5 minutes or until cooked through. Remove fish from pan and allow to cool.

Slice and add the carrots, celery, and one of the onions to the water in the pan. Finely chop the second onion and add it to a bowl with the fish, egg, matzah meal, sugar, and salt and pepper. Using your hands, mash the fish and combine the ingredients together. (If a finer texture is desired, use a food processor to combine ingre-

dients.) Form the fish into 6 to 8 balls. Add these balls to the water, bring the water to simmer, cover, and cook for 1 hour. Serve the gefilte fish on the lettuce with beet horseradish.

Yield: 6 to 8 balls

Creamed Cucumber Slices

1 large cucumber, peeled and sliced
½ red onion, thinly sliced
½ cup plain yogurt
2 tablespoons apple cider vinegar
1 teaspoon sugar
1 tablespoon chopped fresh or 1½ teaspoons dried dill

Combine all ingredients. Mix well. Cover and refrigerate at least 1 hour before serving.

Yield: 4 to 6 servings

Yogurt Cheese Dip

1 8-ounce container plain low fat yogurt
2 teaspoons chopped fresh or ½ teaspoon dried dill
2 teaspoons chopped onion

Line a colander or strainer with several layers of cheese-cloth or a paper coffee filter. Pour the container of yogurt into the lined colander and allow to drain in a bowl overnight in the refrigerator. The remaining yogurt is thick.

Scrape the yogurt into a small bowl and add the dill and onion to it. Serve as a dip or spread.

Yield: ½ cup

Mandel Bread

4 eggs	1 teaspoon baking powder
1 cup sugar	1 cup slivered almonds
½ pound butter, melted	2 tablespoons cocoa powder
1 teaspoon vanilla	cinnamon
3½ cups unbleached flour	sugar

In a medium bowl, beat eggs. Add sugar and mix well. Add melted butter and vanilla. Combine flour and baking powder in a bowl. Add to the egg mixture. Add almonds. Stir until well blended. Divide the dough in half, and to one of the halves add 2 tablespoons cocoa powder.

Now take ⅓ of the vanilla half and ⅓ of the chocolate half and shape them into a long roll about 13 inches long and about 4 inches wide. This is easily done right on a cookie sheet.

Repeat with the remaining dough to form 2 more rolls. Bake for 25 minutes at 350 degrees F. Remove from the oven and slice the rolls into 1-inch slices.

Lay the slices flat on the cookie sheet and sprinkle them with some cinnamon and sugar. Return the mandel bread to the oven for 10 minutes or until slightly browned. Then turn the slices over and sprinkle the other side with cinnamon and sugar and return the mandel bread to the oven for 10 more minutes until this side is also browned.

Remove the cookie sheet from the oven and allow the mandel bread to cool. Store in airtight containers.

Yield: 3 dozen

Red beets with dill.

Red Beets with Dill

2 pounds raw beets
2 medium onions, sliced
½ cup red wine vinegar
1 tablespoon chopped fresh or 1 teaspoon dried dill
1 tablespoon sugar

Wash beets and cut off the greens. Place beets in a pot and cover with water. Bring water to a boil, turn down heat slightly, and cook at boiling until tender, about 20 to 30 minutes.

Allow beets to cool. Save about 1 cup of the cooking liquid. Peel beets and cut into chunks. Place beets in a bowl with remaining ingredients (including the 1 cup of liquid that was set aside). Cover and refrigerate this mixture for several hours or overnight.

Yield: 6 servings

Mandel bread.

CRAFTS

Yarzheit Candles

Part of the Yom Kippur service is a memorial prayer for the dead called Yizkor (literally, "May God Remember"). In addition to reciting this prayer, mourners pledge to give tzedekah, or charity, as a memorial tribute. A Yarzheit candle is lit at sunset and burns until the sunset marking the close of Yom Kippur day. To give the Yom Kippur Yarzheit extra significance, it can be placed in a special ner tamid ("eternal light") to hold the candle.

Materials Needed:

paraffin wax **(approximately 2 pounds)**	**mixing spoon or stick** **wicks (approximately 6**
double boiler	**inches each)**
baking pan	**pencils**
paper cups	

Melting the Wax:

In a double boiler, over a low flame, melt some paraffin, a little bit at a time. The inner pot should be a can or something that you don't mind putting wax in.

Filling the Molds:

Fill the baking pan with cold water and place the paper cups in the pan. Tie one end of each wick to the center of a pencil and balance it over each cup; roll any extra length of wick around the pencil until the wick's end touches the center of the cup's bottom. Carefully pour the melted wax evenly into each cup (see figure 1).

Finishing the Candles:

When the wax is totally hardened, remove the cups and untie the wicks from the pencils. Peel the paper cups away, trim the wicks, and trim any rough edges from the candles.

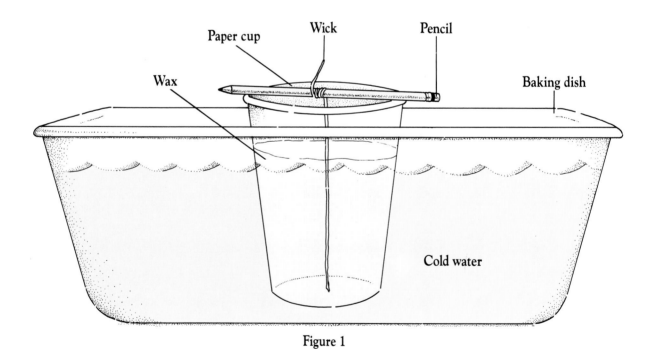

Figure 1

Ner Tamid

Materials Needed:

typing paper and pencil	**4 feet of wire (2 2-foot pieces)**
empty soup can	**Yarzheit candle**
tape	**hook**
hammer and nail	

The Pattern:

Wrap a piece of typing paper around the outside of the soup can. Trim the paper to the height and circumference of the can. Unwrap the paper and draw a picture on it— a Jewish star, for example. Fill the can with water and put it in the freezer. After the water is frozen, rewrap the paper around the can, pattern-side out, and tape it into place. Using a hammer and nail, retrace the pattern by punching holes about ⅛ inch apart in the can. Make sure to include 4 holes spaced evenly apart near the top rim for hanging. Allow the ice to melt in the sink and drain the can.

Hanging the Ner Tamid:

Make hooks on the ends of 2 2-foot lengths of wire by bending their ends around a pencil. Bend each wire in half and attach each to the can on opposite sides of the rim. Place a Yarzheit candle in the can. The ner tamid can now be hung on a hook and lit.

Ner Tamid.

Chapter 4

SUKKOT:
THE FESTIVAL OF
THE BOOTHS

"You shall live in booths seven days . . . in order that future
generations may know that I made the children of Israel
to dwell in booths when I brought them out of the land
of Egypt. . . ."

Leviticus 23: 42–43

Sukkot is one of the three major festivals on the Jewish calendar (Passover and Shavuot are the other two). Sukkot falls exactly two weeks after Rosh Hashanah, and the preparations for it begin immediately after Yom Kippur. It is a colorful holiday, rich with ceremony, commemorating the journey of the children of Israel through the desert after the Exodus from Egypt. During this time, the Israelites were unable to build permanent shelter and so lived in temporary "booths." Sukkot also provides a welcome change of pace from the solemn days of prayer and introspection which accompany Rosh Hashanah and Yom Kippur.

In ancient times, Sukkot was regarded as the outstanding festival of the year, although its appeal in those days may have come about because it was celebrated when the last of the crops were harvested before the onset of winter. It is from this tradition that Sukkot gets one of its nicknames—"The Festival of In-Gathering." Today, Sukkot continues to stress the idea of nature—Jews are commanded to live in natural surroundings for the duration of the festival, giving the holiday its most popular nickname, "The Festival of Booths."

THE SUKKAH

There are many rules that govern living in a sukkah. For the seven days of the festival, Jews are supposed to eat, drink, sleep, and spend leisure time there. It is to be regarded as one's principal abode, the house or apartment as merely a temporary residence. However, according to ancient law, there are certain dispensations for not living in the sukkah. One is excused in case of illness, rain, or severe discomfort. A traveler on the road is excused from eating in a sukkah, as is a person having only light refreshment that does not include bread. Women and children are not required to live in the sukkah. Today, it is still common to eat meals, study, and socialize in the sukkah, but most people no longer sleep in it.

Guests are often invited into the sukkah to share in the meals. The inspiration for this practice is the example of hospitality set by Abraham, who made a habit of asking strangers and passersby to be seated at his table.

Building a Sukkah

As there are rules for living in a sukkah, so, too, are there specific rules governing the construction of the suk-

This sukkah decoration features zodiacal and religious symbols.

kah. (However, it is not necessary to bless the construction of the sukkah, since the religious duty is not in building it, but in *living* in it.)

The Roof   The temporary quality of the sukkah lies in the roofing material used, which must meet the following rules: It must grow from the earth (as opposed to being mined); it must be cut down and no longer be connected to the ground; and it must not be subject to ritual impurity (such as animal skins). Known collectively as *sekhakh*, sukkahs' roof materials typically include branches cut from trees or bushes, straw, cornstalks, bamboo reeds, and narrow wooden beams. Fruits and food, metal, cloth, or attached tree branches are not permitted. The roof must be attached after the walls are completed. It must provide more shade than sunlight, yet the roof materials must not be so thick that they do not let the rain in. It must be open enough for stars to be seen through it, but any opening may not exceed approximately eleven inches in width or length. Any sukkah built indoors, or under the overhang of a balcony, porch, or under a tree is invalid.

The Walls   No restrictions apply to the materials used for the walls of the sukkah. They can be wood, metal, canvas, stone, or brick. However, there must be at least two complete walls, with the third wall a minimum width of 3⅝ inches. The fourth side of the sukkah may be left completely open. The common practice today is to build four walls, with an open doorway for an entrance. When a sukkah is built adjacent to a permanent structure, one or more of the walls of that structure may be used.

The minimum height a sukkah may be is thirty-five inches; the maximum height is thirty-five feet, three inches. Though it may have permanent walls, every sukkah must qualify as a temporary dwelling, in keeping with a holiday commemorating the wanderings of the Israelites after their Exodus from Egypt. A sukkah can be built to hold only one person, or it can be large enough to hold the entire congregation of a synagogue or, as in Israel, an entire kibbutz population.

Decorations   The roof and walls of the sukkah are usually decorated with flowers, fruit, nuts, gourds, pictures, and tapestries. The Talmud indicates that nuts, pomegranates, and grape clusters were all hung from the roof of the sukkah in ancient times.

THE FOUR SPECIES

The four species (in Hebrew the *arba'ah minim*) consist of the *etrog* (citron), *lulav* (palm branch), *hadas* (myrtle twig), and *aravah* (willow). As the Torah commands: "And ye shall take you on the first day the fruit of godly trees, branches of palm-trees, and boughs of thick trees, and willows of the brook and ye shall rejoice before the Lord your God seven days" (Leviticus 23:40).

The four species symbolize many things. As agricultural symbols they signify the final harvest and the fertility of the land. They also provide a connection with the soil, even in an urban environment. The four species have also been said to relate to four types of people: The etrog possesses both taste and good odor; the palm possesses only taste; the myrtle only odor; and the willow has neither quality. Similarly, some Jews have both knowledge and good works to their name; some have only the former; some have just the latter; and some have neither. Therefore, as the Jews come together to worship and rejoice before God, the failings of one person are compensated for by the virtues of the others.

Finally, to hold these particular plants in hand is to identify with the Land of Israel, as they are all found

Above: During Sukkot, the lulav can be purchased in open markets. Opposite page: This etrog container is made of cast silver and carved wood.

there. It is believed that these four species were chosen because of their staying power—they will stay fresh and moist for the seven days of Sukkot.

The Ritual of the Four Species

There is a proper way to celebrate with the four species. First, three myrtle twigs and two willows are tied to the lulav, with the myrtle set slightly higher than the willow. Once this is done, they are to be set into a holder made from a palm leaf slipped onto the lulav. Holding the entire unit in the right hand, side-by-side with the etrog in the left, one recites the traditional blessing: "Blessed is the Lord our God, Ruler of the universe, by Whose mitzvot we are hallowed, Who give us the mitzvah of Lulav."

The proper way to hold the lulav is with the spine facing the holder. Hold the etrog with the *pitom* (nipple) on top and the stem or stalk where it had been attached to the tree on the bottom. At several times during the service the lulav and the etrog are pointed three times in all directions, accompanied by a slight shaking or waving of the lulav. This is known as *na'anuim* and symbolizes the presence of God in all directions: three times back and forth to the east, then three times toward the south, west, north, upward, and downward. The ritual is to be observed every day of Sukkot, except for the Sabbath.

Choosing the Lulav and Etrog The lulav and etrog should be chosen by the person who will be using them. It is not permissible to borrow a lulav or etrog from

שבעת זמן מתן תורתנו

Above: During Simchat Torah, the torah scrolls are removed from the ark and carried around in a procession. Opposite page: These flags are carried during the procession.

someone else. Extra care must be taken to choose an etrog as close to perfection as possible. The beauty of an etrog is not judged solely by size, but by how evenly shaped it is, whether it has blemishes or spots, and by the convolutions of its skin. Certain flaws render an etrog unfit for ritual use. These include the presence of a hole or perforation; a missing part; a broken or missing pitom; scarring; dryness, peeling, or splitting; and roundness, making the etrog seem more like a ball.

Artistic Traditions

The etrog container is one of the ritual objects to which artists have devoted considerable talent. Old kiddush cups created specifically for this holiday have been found, as have Sukkot decorations on floor mosaics of ancient synagogues.

SIMCHAT TORAH

Simchat Torah, Hebrew for "Rejoicing of the Torah," falls on the ninth day of Sukkot and is a gleeful celebration that proclaims the completion of the cycle of reading the Torah and its immediate recommencement. The Torah scrolls are removed from the ark and carried around in a ceremonial procession known as *hakkafot.*

On Simchat Torah, many synagogues hold a special ceremony for children entering religious school for the first time. This ceremony, called consecration, emphasizes the importance of learning the Torah. It is customary to present each child with a miniature Torah scroll.

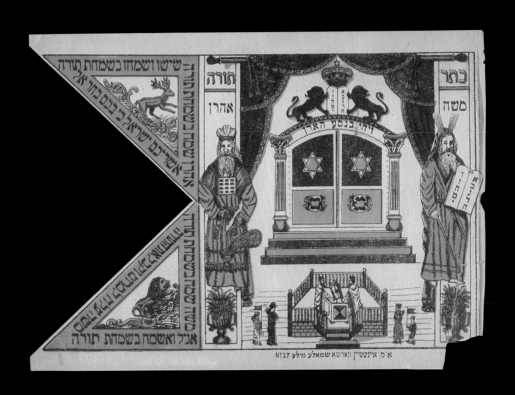

MENU: SUKKOT EVE SUPPER IN THE SUKKAH

Baked Haddock with Mustard Sauce

Spinach, Mushrooms, and Barley

Sweet Potato and Carrot Tzimmes

Marinated Fresh Vegetables

Apple Coffeecake

Baked Haddock with Mustard Sauce

> 1 pound haddock fillet
> 2 tablespoons light mayonnaise
> 2 tablespoons coarse mustard
> 2 teaspoons horseradish

Place the fish in a baking pan. Combine mayonnaise, mustard, and horseradish. Spread over the fish in the pan. Bake at 350 degrees F for 15 minutes or until the fish is opaque throughout.

Yield: 4 servings

Spinach, Mushrooms, and Barley

> 1 cup barley
> 3 cups water or vegetable stock
> 2 cups sliced fresh mushrooms
> 3 cups chopped fresh spinach, not packed

Put barley, water, and chicken stock in a 4-quart pot. Bring the water to a boil, turn down heat to simmer, cover, and cook for 45 minutes.

Meanwhile, wash and slice mushrooms and then add to pot while it is cooking.

Wash and chop spinach and add to pot, leaving about 10 minutes cooking time.

After 45 minutes, all the water should be absorbed into the barley and it should be soft. If not, cook an additional 10 minutes and then serve.

Yield: 4 cups

Sweet Potato and Carrot Tzimmes

A tzimmes *is a mixture of anything, but where food is concerned, it seems to be the consensus that sweet potatoes are part of the combination.*

> 2 cups water
> 1 pound carrots, peeled and sliced
> 2 sweet potatoes, peeled and sliced
> ½ cup large pitted prunes
> ¼ cup apricots

Add all the ingredients to a pot. Bring water to a boil, then lower heat to simmer, cover, and cook for 1 hour (see note) or until the water is absorbed and the potatoes and carrots are soft, almost mushy.

Yield: 6 to 8 servings

Note: This dish can be prepared easily in the microwave. Use only 1 cup of water with all remaining ingredients and add to a microwavable bowl, cover, and microwave on high for 5 minutes. Stir the mixture, rotate bowl, re-cover, and microwave an additional 9 to 10 minutes. Let tzimmes stand an additional 2 to 4 minutes before serving.

Apple Coffeecake

½ pound stick margarine, softened
1 cup sugar
3 eggs
1 teaspoon vanilla
1 teaspoon baking soda
2 teaspoons baking powder
2½ cups unbleached flour
1 cup plain yogurt
3 apples, peeled and sliced
2 teaspoons cinnamon
¼ cup sugar
1 cup chopped walnuts

Apple coffeecake.

In a large bowl, cream together the stick margarine and the cup of sugar until light and fluffy. Add the eggs one at a time and beat well after each. Add the vanilla.

Combine the baking soda, baking powder, and flour in a bowl. Add this dry mixture to the egg mixture alternately with the yogurt. Beat well after each addition.

Spray a 9-inch tube pan (angel food pan) with non-stick spray. Add half the batter to the pan, spreading over the bottom. Spread half the sliced apples over the batter. Combine the cinnamon, ¼ cup of sugar, and walnuts and spread half the mixture over the apples. Cover this with the remaining batter. Add the remaining apples and the remaining nut mixture. Bake at 375 degrees F for 45 minutes. Cool slightly in the pan before removing and cutting.

Yield: 1 9-inch cake

CRAFTS

Sukkah Walls

The Jews of Bible times lived in tents while wandering in the desert for forty years. The sukkah is reminiscent of those tents, though it is much more spacious in order to encourage group participation while celebrating the harvest festival of Sukkot. In order to build a sukkah, a frame built out of 2 × 4-inch boards might be simplest. The sukkah should not be more than 10 to 12 inches off the ground, and the walls must be between 35 inches and 35 feet in height (not lower or higher). After an appropriate frame is built, the walls can be attached. Aluminum, canvas, fiberglass, or some decorative cloth are all possible materials.

Note: The size of the sukkah depends on how long your 2 × 4-inch boards are. The height of each wall must be equal. Boards opposite one another on each frame must be equal, too.

Materials Needed:

2 × 4-inch boards	**sheets or other large pieces of cloth**
nails	**tacks**
hammer	**joist plates**

For Each Wall Build a Frame:

Use 4 2 × 4-inch boards to construct each wall. Cut each end of every 2 × 4 at 45-degree angles toward each other. Construct a frame by joining the 4 boards with nails (see figure 1).

Covering the Frames:

You'll need a piece of cloth slightly bigger than each frame for each wall. Stretch the cloth over each frame. Nail in tacks, starting from the center of each board (see figure 2), and work your way outward. Alternate sides to keep the fabric taut. Finally, join the walls with joist plates.

Decorating a Sukkah:

Decorating a sukkah is really a personal matter. Since Sukkot is a harvest holiday, hang fruit, autumn leaves, and gourds. Paintings and chains made especially for the holiday are also favorites.

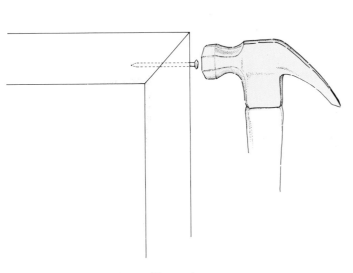

Figure 1

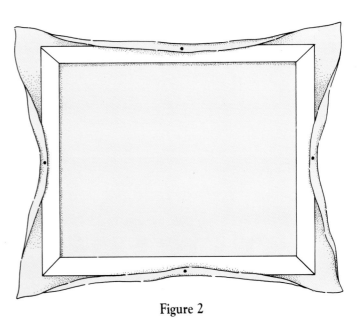

Figure 2

Paper Bead Chains

Materials Needed:

    magazines   pencil
    scissors   thread
    glue

Making the Beads:

Cut long thin triangles (about 1 inch wide and 8 inches long) from colorful magazine pictures. Begin wrapping a triangle around a pencil, starting with the base, and continue until there is only about 2 inches left. Put glue on the underside of the triangle's point and finish wrapping; the glue should keep the bead from unravelling. Gently slide the bead off the pencil and let it dry.

Stringing the Beads:

If you like, you can string the beads one after another in the usual fashion. For something a little more complicated and unique, cut a length of thread and string a bead in the center of it; this will be the end of your chain. Cross the ends of the thread and string the next bead twice—once with each thread going in opposite directions (see figure 1). Add as many beads as you like, always remembering to cross the ends of the thread and string the beads once from either direction.

Cloth Bead Chains

Materials Needed:

scraps of fabric (any color, pattern, or texture), cut to 3 inches wide and at least 10 inches long
needle and thread
polyester fill
rug needle and embroidery floss or heavy thread

The Beads:

Fold a length of fabric in half with the wrong, or "back," side out. Run a backstitch seam 2 inches away from the fold to form a long 2-inch tube. Cut the fabric into smaller, 3-inch tubes. Now, turn a tube inside out so the right side is out. Place a small amount of polyester fill inside it. Make a running stitch around one side, pull both sides of the thread (like a drawstring) and make a knot. You can tuck the edges in or leave them out before closing the sides. Do the same on the other end of the bead. Sew the other beads using the same method.

Stringing the Beads:

When your beads are finished, use a rug needle and heavy thread to string them. Carefully work the needle through each bead lengthwise.

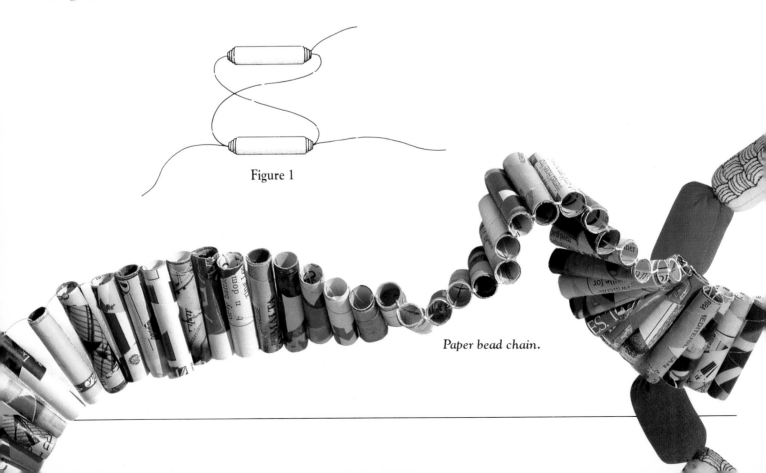

Figure 1

Paper bead chain.

SIMCHAT TORAH CRAFTS

The process of beginning and ending the year's Torah readings is celebrated with seven hakkafot, or processional circuits, of a synogogue's congregants. The Torah scrolls are paraded around the inside of the synagogue to bring everyone, especially children, closer to the Torah. While the procession continues, it is customary for the children to wave flags.

Simchat Torah Flags

Materials Needed:

felt	glitter
glue	thin wooden dowels (chopsticks work well)

The Flag:

Cut felt into a triangle, making sure the base is the shortest side and the other two sides are equal. Use glue, glitter, and other colors of felt to decorate it.

Attaching It to the Pole:

Put glue along the base of the triangle and wrap it tightly around one end of a dowel. Allow it to dry completely.

Simchat torah flag.

Cloth bead chains.

Chapter 5

CHANUKAH:
THE FESTIVAL OF LIGHTS

"... who has sanctified us with His commandments and
commanded us to kindle the lights of Chanukah."

Chanukah prayer

Chanukah is an eight-day festival that, like most other Jewish holidays, has both historic and seasonal origins. It celebrates the victory of the Maccabees over the Hellenistic Syrians in 165 B.C.E.—the triumph of Jewish over Greek values—and the miracle of the oil for the *menorah* in the Holy Temple lasting not one, but eight days. By that year, too, the celebration of a winter holiday had been a long-standing Hebrew tradition, marking the gradual increase in daylight after the short, cold, and ominous days of fall. An ancient Jewish custom dictated that a fire be kindled at the temple altar during this season. Thus, the central motif of Chanukah has always been light: the light of the altar, the light everlasting, and the eight candles of the menorah. In fact, the only mitzvah associated with Chanukah is the kindling of the lights each night of this celebration.

Chanukah is the only important Jewish festival not referred to in the Bible. Nonetheless, during this holiday the Torah is read every day from Numbers 7 to 8, which describe the offerings brought to the consecrated altar in the wilderness by the chief of each tribe of Israel.

CUSTOMS

Lighting the menorah is just one of the many Chanukah customs handed down from generation to generation.

Food

During Chanukah, it is traditional to eat dairy foods and foods cooked in oil; the former to commemorate the story of Judith and Holofernes (see page 76); the oil to remember the eternal miracle of the holiday. In eastern Europe, Chanukah food includes *latkes*, potato pancakes fried in oil. In Israel, the custom is to eat fried doughnuts called *sufganiyot* (see page 80).

The Dreidl

After the latkes and sufganiyot have been consumed, games of chance are often played. The most popular is *dreidl*, a derivative of an old German gambling game, played with a four-sided top containing a letter on each side. Each letter stands for one word of the phrase "A great miracle happened there (here)." The "nun" stands for *nes*, or "miracle"; the "gimmel" stands for *gadol*, or "great"; the "heh" stands for *ha-i-yah*, or "happened"; and the "shin" stands for *sham*, or "there." If you happen to be playing the game in Israel, the last letter would be a "pay," standing for *po*, which means "here" (a great miracle happened here).

How to play dreidl To play dreidl, each player starts with ten pennies (or ten pieces of chocolate *gelt*, ten nuts, ten raisins, etc.). Each player puts one penny in the pot. The dreidl is spun by one player at a time. If the dreidl lands on nun, he or she does nothing. If the dreidl lands on gimmel, the player takes everything in the pot. If the dreidl lands on heh, the player takes half of the pot. If the dreidl lands on shin or po, the player must add two pennies to the pot. When one or no pennies are left in the pot, each player adds one. When one person has won everything, the game is over.

Chanukah Gelt

There is an old, widespread custom of giving children Chanukah gelt (money) to spread the light and joy of the holiday and to hasten the coming of the Messiah. More

Opposite page: Dreidl is a game enjoyed by young and old alike. Above: This chanukah menorah is made from cast and engraved silver.

recently, the custom has changed, and most children are given presents each night of the holiday.

The Book of Judith

The Hebrew word for Chanukah has its root in the word "study." Thus, Chanukah is a time when issues relating to Jewish education are addressed. The Book of Judith is often discussed as a symbol of both learning and of the holiday itself. The story of Judith symbolizes the victory of the Jews over the Hellenistic Syrians. Judith, a Jewish woman, fed the Syrian general Holofernes great amounts of cheese, causing him to become very thirsty. To quench his thirst, Judith gave him large quantities of wine. The general fell into a drunken stupor, enabling Judith to cut off his head. This in turn struck fear into the Syrians, and they fled.

The Prayers

Three prayers are said during the festival of Chanukah. One is recited only on the first night and recalls the ancient Jewish custom of giving thanks for the increasing daylight hours: "Blessed are You, Lord our God, King of the Universe, who has granted us life and sustenance and permitted us to reach this season."

The other two prayers are said on each of the other seven nights of Chanukah: "Blessed are You, Lord our God, King of the Universe, who has sanctified us with His Commandments and commanded us to kindle the light of Chanukah"; and "Blessed are You, Lord our God, King of the Universe, who performed miracles for our fathers in those days, at this time."

The Chanukah Candles

There are many rules concerning the lighting of Chanukah candles. Each person in the household, male and female, should light his or her own candles. The candles (either wax or oil can be used) should be lit on each night of the eight-day holiday. They should be placed in a window facing the street, on the opposite side of the

The shamash usually stands out on the Chanukah menorah.

doorway from the *mezuzah*, so that passersby can see the light coming from the window and recognize what night of the celebration it is. The candles should be lit soon after sundown and should burn for at least a half hour. Unlike Shabbat custom, the light from Chanukah candles should not be used for any purpose.

How to light the candles   The accepted practice is to light one candle on the first day of the festival, two candles on the second day, and so on, plus the *shamash*, or "head" candle. The candles should be placed in the menorah beginning from right and moving left. Light the shamash and recite the proper blessings. Then light the candles with the shamash, moving from left to right. Once all of the candles are lit, place the shamash in the menorah's special shamash holder.

Since the celebration of Chanukah lasts for eight days, it will coincide with Shabbat at least once. On those days, the Chanukah candles should be lit before the Shabbat candles. On Saturday, the Chanukah candles should be lit before the havdalah candle if they are lit in the temple or synagogue; if the candles are lit at home, light the havdalah candle first.

Once the candles are lit, it is customary to sing two songs: "*Ha Nerot Halalu*" ("We Kindle These Lights") and "*Maos Tsur*" ("Rock of Ages").

In Turkey, it was customary to make candle wicks from the fibers in which the etrog was wrapped for Sukkot. Following Chanukah, the candle remains were formed into another candle that was to be used to search for leaven before Passover.

The Artistic Tradition

As with other Jewish holidays and festivals, Jewish artisans and craftsmen honed their skills creating beautiful objects with which to celebrate Chanukah. Most notable are the menorahs, many of which were made in precious metals—silver and gold—filigreed with intricate designs and sayings. Dreidls, too, allowed these artists to fashion things of beauty and joy for children. Most driedls were made from wood and metals.

Maos Tsur (Rock of Ages)

Rock of ages, let our song
Praise Thy saving power;
Thou, amidst the raging foes,
Was our sheltering tower.
Furious they assailed us,
But thine will availed us;
    And Thy word,
    Broke their sword
When our own strength failed us.

Children of the martyr race,
Whether free or fettered,
Wake the echoes of the songs,
Where you may be scattered.
Yours the message cheering
That the time is nearing
Which will see
All peoples free,
Tyrants disappearing.

MENU: CHANUKAH FOOD

Red Beet Borscht

Potato Latkes with Sour Cream and Applesauce

Green Salad with Chunky Tuna, Cheese, Celery, and Sunflower Seeds

Sufganiyot (Jelly Doughnuts)

Red Beet Borscht

5 large beets (about 2½ pounds)	¼ cup lemon juice
4 cups water	2 to 4 tablespoons sugar
1 onion	sour cream
2 bay leaves	

Wash the beets thoroughly, cut off ends, and add to an 8-quart pot with the water. Cook the beets until tender, about 45 minutes. Remove the beets from the pot, saving the liquid. Measure the liquid and add enough water to make 6 cups.

Peel and grate the beets. Put the beets back into the pot with the liquid. Cut the onion into quarters and add to the pot along with the bay leaves, lemon juice, and sugar to taste. Cook for an additional 20 minutes. Remove the onion and the bay leaves. Chill. Serve with sour cream.

Yield: 8 to 10 servings

Potato Latkes with Sour Cream and Applesauce

5 medium potatoes	¼ teaspoon baking powder
1 small onion	corn or peanut oil
¼ cup unbleached flour	applesauce
1 egg, beaten	sour cream

Shred the potatoes with a hand grater or food processor and place in a bowl. Grate the onion and add it to the potatoes. Add the flour, beaten egg, and baking powder.

Heat some of the oil in a large heavy skillet. For each latke, drop about ¼ cup of the potato mixture in a mound. Brown on one side and then turn, flatten, and brown the other side. Remove the finished latke to a paper-towel-lined plate to drain. Continue making the latkes, adding more oil if necessary. The latkes can be kept warm by putting them in a baking pan in the oven on low heat.

Serve with applesauce and sour cream.

Yield: 16 latkes

Green Salad with Chunky Tuna, Cheese, Celery, and Sunflower Seeds

12 red-leaf lettuce leaves
1 can (6½ ounces) water-packed tuna
4 ounces Swiss cheese
2 stalks celery, sliced
3 tablespoons sunflower seeds

Wash lettuce, tear, and add to a salad bowl. Drain tuna, break up into chunks, and add to the bowl. Cut Swiss cheese into ½-inch cubes and add to salad. Add the celery and the sunflower seeds. Top with your favorite dressing, toss, and serve.

Yield: 4 servings

Sufganiyot.

Sufganiyot (Jelly Doughnuts)

2 eggs	½ teaspoon salt
½ cup sugar	1 cup milk
1 tablespoon vegetable oil	¼ teaspoon vanilla
2¾ cups unbleached flour	strawberry jam
1½ teaspoons baking powder	powdered sugar

Beat the eggs. Add the sugar and the oil and beat again. Combine the flour, baking powder, and salt in a separate bowl. Add half of this to the egg mixture and beat well. Add the milk and vanilla and then the remaining flour mixture. More flour may be needed to form a soft dough that can be rolled. Refrigerate the dough for 1 hour.

Roll out the dough to ¼ inch thickness. Cut circles of dough with a glass to form 32 circles (about 2 inches in diameter). On half of the circles place a teaspoon of jam. Then place another circle of dough over each one and pinch the edges together.

Deep fry the doughnuts in hot oil using a thermometer to keep the oil at 350 degrees F. When doughnuts are golden, remove them from the oil with a slotted spoon and place on paper towels to drain. The doughnuts can be rolled in powdered sugar.

Yield: 16 sufganiyot

CRAFTS

Chanukia

Ever since the victory of Judah the Maccabee and his brothers over the Syrians, chanukiot (another name for menorahs) have been used to signify the miracle of the oil burning for eight days instead of one day, as was expected. The earliest chanukiot were small clay lamps and were kept outdoors to publicize the miracle. However, the display aroused hostility from pagan fire worshippers who lived amongst the Jews. As a result, rabbis permitted the chanukiot to be kept indoors. Now, no longer subject to weather conditions, the possibilities for chanukiot have become much more varied and often reflect the culture of their locales.

Today, many chanukiot hold candles rather than oil. The most important consideration when making a chanukia is that it must allow for nine flames. In addition, you must make sure that each flame burns distinctly from its neighboring flames.

Materials Needed:
FIMO or self-hardening clay (approximately ½ pound)
Chanukah candle
household cement

The Pieces:
Roll 11 small spheres with the FIMO or self-hardening clay. Press the Chanukah candle into each sphere to create holders for the candles. Then roll a long snake using more FIMO or clay.

Hardening:
If you're using clay, spread out the pieces and let them dry overnight. FIMO must be baked in an oven to harden.

Assembling:
Using household cement, glue 9 of the holders onto the snake with even amounts of space between them. Stack and glue the remaining 2 holders on top of the first holder; this will be for the shamash. Make sure the cement is completely dry before using your chanukia.

For Variety:
Paint your chanukia or use different colored clays or FIMO.

A chanukia.

Cloth Dreidl

It's believed that dreidls were invented during the time of Antiochus in order to be used as a surreptitious study aid. Jews were forbidden to study the Torah during that period, and although the dreidl's letters taught some Hebrew, a game of dreidl seemed perfectly unthreatening to the enemy. This dreidl is not for the game but is an appropriate item to fill with Chanukah gifts!

Materials Needed:

¼ yard each of contrasting fabrics (A and B)
ruler
scissors
fabric crayon
brown bag
pencil
pins
file cards measuring 5 × 8 inches
¼ yard single-thickness quilt batting

You may use a zig-zag sewing machine or hand appliqué technique for this project.

Cutting:

Cut 4 squares of fabric A and 6 squares of fabric B, 4½ inches each, and set aside. Cut out the triangle pattern in its actual size from the brown bag and copy this outline 4 times on both fabric A and B. Allow ¼ inch all around for seaming. Set aside. Cut out the letter patterns in their actual size from the file cards. Trace 2 of the letters (nun and heh) on fabric A and the other 2 on fabric B. Now cut out 4 squares, 4 inches each, from the brown bag to use for stiffening the fabric squares when the letters are sewn on. Cut 4 triangles (using the pattern) and 5 squares of quilt batting, 4 inches each. Trace and cut the handle pattern from either fabric.

Sewing:

Place a fabric letter in the center of an opposite color fabric square. Hold a paper square behind the fabric square and sew the letter on. Turn the square over and trim the excess paper. After all 4 letters are complete, place batting between fabric squares with letters on them and plain squares of the same fabric. For each panel, stitch around the batting, leaving the top open. Each square should now be 4 inches. Use the same method for triangles and the remaining square (fabric B). Hand stitch the triangles to the squares, and also stitch the squares to each other, making certain to keep the sides in order (nun, gimmel, heh, shin). Now, stitch the handle into a tube and stitch a circle of fabric onto the top. Stuff it tightly with batting and stitch it onto the center of the remaining square. Sew the top of the dreidl on one side only. You can use a button or a hook to close it if you like.

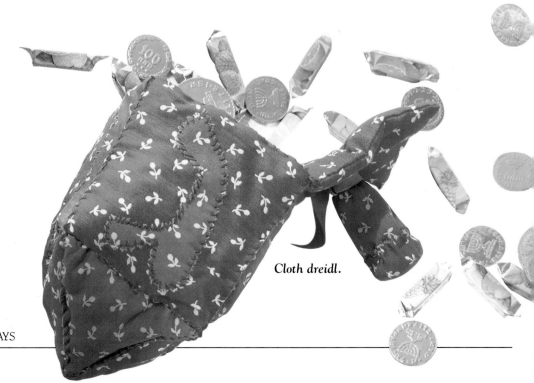

Cloth dreidl.

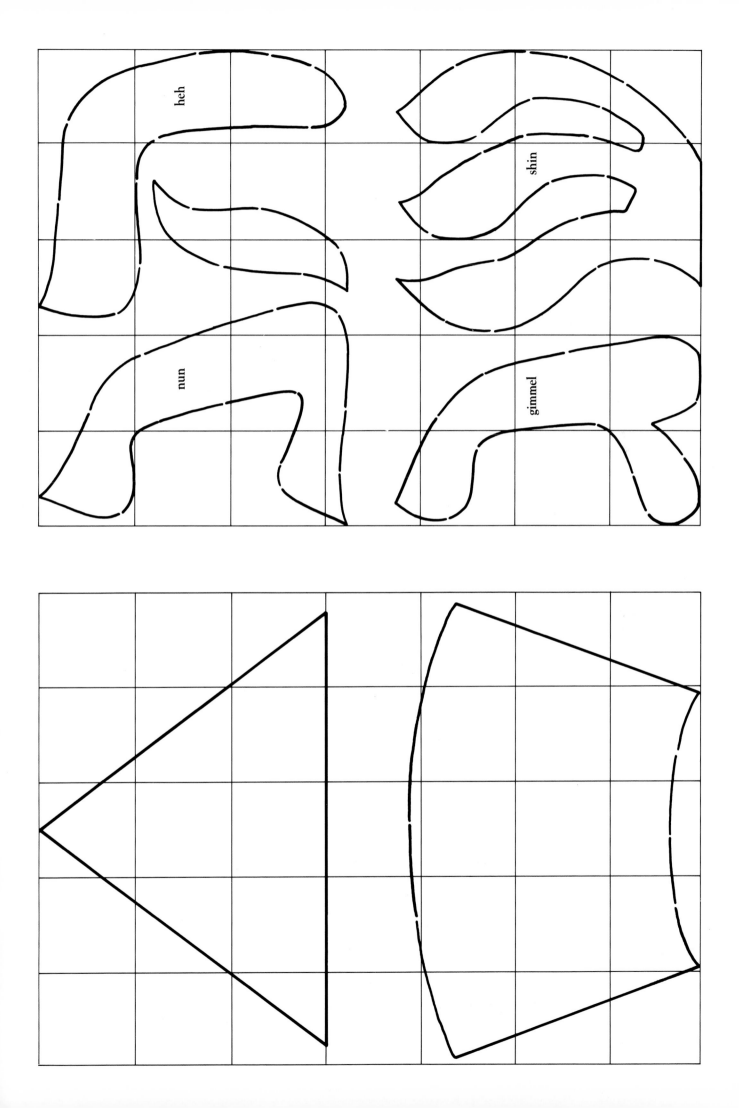

Chapter 6

PURIM: THE FEAST OF LOTS

"And it was so, when the king saw Esther the queen . . . she obtained favor in his sight and the king held out to Esther the golden sceptre that was in his hand."

Esther 5:2

*This diorama shows Esther kneeling in front of King
Ahashuerus.*

urim, the Feast of Lots, celebrates the victory of the Jewish community in Persia, led by Queen Esther and her cousin Mordechai, over a plot to exterminate them that had been formulated by Prime Minister Haman and King Ahashuerus. Haman had cast *pur*, or "lots," to determine the date of the Jews' annihilation, but Esther convinced the king not to go ahead with Haman's plan. In fact, the king had Haman killed instead! In commemoration of this event, Jews gather to read the story of Esther and to celebrate.

While Purim is supposedly purely historical in origin, it falls close to the same time as other holidays, namely the Christian Carnivale, and to the emergence of spring. During Purim, it is traditional for children and adults to dress up as Mordechai, Esther, Haman, and Ahashuerus

and parade around. Like Purim, Carnivale includes wild revelry, hilarity, masquerades, and plays.

The day before Purim is a fast day—called the Fast of Esther—that begins at sunrise. This is unusual, as all other fast days on the Jewish calendar begin with sunset the night before.

The central elements of this holiday are joy and celebration. In fact, Purim is a time of general good-feeling towards everyone, a time when it is considered a mitzvah to drink, drink, drink—to drink so much that it is impossible to distinguish the difference between blessed Mordechai and cursed Haman.

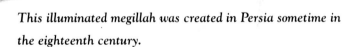

This illuminated megillah was created in Persia sometime in the eighteenth century.

The reading of the Megillah is done much like a play, with different voices used and improvised dramatics accompanying the text. The most famous, and fun, part of the reading involves the blotting out of Haman's name: Everywhere it appears, the congregation is supposed to yell, make noise, stamp the feet, or use a noisemaker called a *gregar*. It is important to remember, however, that a mitzvah involved with reading the Megillah stipulates that every single word must be heard. Therefore, the reader should always wait until the Haman-inspired noise has died down before continuing with the reading.

It is also mentioned in the Megillah that the poor should be helped on Purim, to remind us that no happiness or joy is possible unless everyone can be a part of it. Thus, it is a mitzvah to give presents to at least two poor people. Related to this is the custom of *shalakhmones*, in which everyone is supposed to send presents of at least two kinds of fruit, cookies, and candies to at least one friend.

WHAT TO EAT AT PURIM

There are several foods associated with the celebration of Purim. The most popular is *hamantaschen*, the three-cornered dough cookie most often filled with poppy seeds, jam, or cheese. *Kreplach*, a three-cornered, meat-filled dough pastry, is another favorite. The triangular shape of both delicacies represents the shape of Haman's hat.

THE ARTISTIC TRADITION

As previously mentioned, an unusual aspect of the story of Esther is the complete absence of the word "God" in the Megillah. This has allowed Jewish artists a freedom previously unknown to actually tell a story and include the characters of the story. Beautifully illuminated Megillahs abound, and many are quite old. Masks to be used during the celebration of the holiday are another item made and brightly decorated.

THE MA'ARIV SERVICE

The *Ma'ariv* service marks the beginning of the Purim festivities. This service is a spoof of other services of the year, using melodies of songs from other holidays and changing them by exaggerating them or putting them in unexpected places. Before the service, or before reading the *Megillah*, which contains the story of Esther, it is customary to collect a half *shekel* from each celebrant in remembrance of the half-shekel tax collected in biblical times from every adult male to support the temple. This money is then given to charity.

The Megillah

The Megillah is read at the end of the Ma'ariv service and again the next morning. Traditionally, the Megillah was written on parchment with a wood winder at one end. An interesting aspect of the Megillah, and the story of Esther, is that it does not mention God at all, allowing it to be highly decorated with pictures.

This charming mask (above and opposite page) contains the faces of three of the characters in the Purim story: Queen Esther, wicked Haman, and King Ahashuerus.

MENU: PURIM EVE SUPPER

Beef and Rice Stuffed Cabbage

Noodle Kugel

Fresh Fruit Salad

Hamantaschen

Beef and Rice Stuffed Cabbage

> 1 large head of cabbage
> 1½ pounds ground chuck
> ¼ cup plus 2 tablespoons uncooked rice
> 1 onion, grated
> 3 onions, sliced
> 1 can Italian tomatoes (28 ounces)
> ½ cup brown sugar
> ¼ cup vinegar
> ¼ cup lemon juice

Remove some of the cabbage heart with a vegetable corer. Place the cabbage in a large pot and pour boiling water over it. Cover the pot and allow to stand about 30 minutes, until the leaves soften. Separate the leaves and spread them on a towel.

Blend the meat, rice, and grated onion. Place a tablespoon of this mixture in the center of a cabbage leaf and roll the leaf so that the meat is securely inside.

Continue preparing cabbage rolls until there is no more meat mixture.

Slice the remaining cabbage and add it to the bottom of a large, heavy pot. Add sliced onion. Place the cabbage rolls on top. Pour the tomatoes, sugar, vinegar, and lemon juice over the rolls. Cover and bake at 300 degrees F for 3 hours.

Yield: 12 servings

Noodle Kugel

> ½ pound broad egg noodles
> 2 eggs
> 1 egg white
> 1 can crushed pineapple (8 ounces)
>
> 1 tablespoon sugar
> ½ teaspoon cinnamon
> dash salt

Boil noodles in water for 10 minutes, drain, and combine with remaining ingredients. Pour into greased 8 × 8-inch baking dish. Bake at 300 degrees F for 1 hour. Kugel should be brown and crispy on top. Cut kugel into squares before serving.

Yield: 9 servings

Hamantaschen

> ¼ pound pareve margarine
> ½ cup sugar
> 2 eggs
> 2½ cups unbleached flour
>
> 1½ teaspoons baking powder
> ¼ teaspoon salt
> apricot pastry
>   (or other) filling

Preheat oven to 350 degrees F. Cream margarine and sugar until fluffy. Add eggs and combine well. Mix flour, baking powder, and salt into mixture with a spoon.

When well mixed, form into 2 balls and wrap each with plastic wrap or waxed paper and refrigerate for several hours or overnight.

Roll out one of the balls to a circle about 10 inches in diameter. Using a glass or round biscuit or cookie cutter with a 2½-inch diameter, cut approximately 15 circles out of the ball of dough. Repeat with the other ball.

Top each cookie with a teaspoon of filling in the center of the circle. Then form a hamantaschen by squeezing the cookie up in 3 places to form a triangle. Some popular fillings are apricot, prune (lekvar), poppy seed, almond paste, or jelly. These fillings are usually commercial products such as the Baker brand ready-to-use cake and pastry filling. Bake for 30 minutes.

Yield: 30 hamantaschen

CRAFTS

Shalakhmones Sacks

The Book of Esther (9:22) says that Purim should be observed by "days of feasting and gladness, and of sending portions to one another. . . ." From this arose the custom of giving shalakhmones. Giving these gifts of food has become a popular tradition. Typically, baskets are filled with hamantaschen, fruit, and other goodies.

Materials needed:

> **piece of cloth 15 × 40 inches**
> **needle and thread**
> **iron**
> **safety pin**
> **20-inch piece of rope**
> **piece of cardboard 9½ × 5½ inches**

The Sack:

Fold down 2 inches of the 15-inch edge of the cloth. Make sure the wrong side is down and iron a crease. Do the same of the other side. Now sew a loose hem 1 inch away from the edge using back stitch.

Fold the cloth in half lengthwise 15 × 20 inches with the wrong-side out. Using backstitch again, sew the sides together from the fold to the bottom of the hem you've made at the top. You don't want to sew the top shut.

The Drawstring:

The bag you've created is inside-out. Turn it to the right side. Attach the safety pin to an end of the rope and work it through the hole created by the seams at the top of the bag. Continue all the way around. Tie the ends of the rope together in a tight knot and pull the rope upward at both openings in the hem.

The Bottom:

Before packing the shalakhmones sack with your goodies, put the piece of cardboard in the bottom to help it stand better.

Gregar

When the Megillah (The Book of Esther) is read, it is traditional to drown out the name of the villain, Haman, by stamping, yelling, and using noisemakers.

Materials needed:
- popping corn
- pencil
- large empty juice can (with only 2 holes at the top that were used for pouring)
- cardboard
- scissors
- colored felt (at least 8 × 24 inches of a color)
- household cement
- glue

To Make the Noise:

Put a handful of popping corn into the can through the 2 holes. Trace the base of the can onto the cardboard. Cut the cardboard and trim the circle so it fits snugly onto the side of the can with the holes.

Decorating the Can:

Trace the base twice onto the large piece of felt and cut each circle so that it is about 1 inch larger all the way around. You'll need darts in the felt to stretch it over the ends, so cut them about every 2 inches to the correct size of the circle (see figure 1). Glue the felt over each end using household cement. Wrap the rest of the can with more felt, trim it, and glue it to the can as well. Decorate the gregar using glue and other colors of felt or, if your gregar is a light color, use markers and paint.

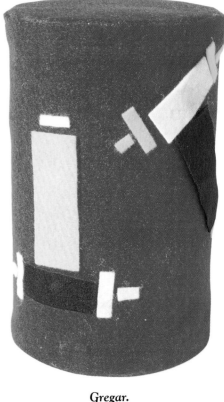

Gregar.

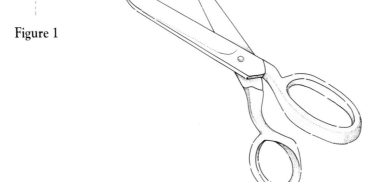

Figure 1

Purim Mask

A crucial theme in the Purim story is that of mistaken identity and may be the source of the tradition of masquerading on Purim. The wearing of masks and costumes is a tradition on this holiday.

Materials needed:
  balloon
  glue
  water
  newspaper
  paints and paint brush
  construction paper, aluminum foil, glitter, cotton balls
    (or other decorations)
  yarn

The Base:

Blow up a balloon so that it is a little larger than the head of whomever will be wearing the mask. In a bowl, combine 1 part glue to about 4 parts warm water and mix thoroughly. Cut strips of newspaper about 1 inch wide and soak them one at a time in the glue mixture and wrap them around the balloon. Cover the balloon completely with 2 layers of newspaper. Let it dry (probably overnight).

The Face:

When the balloon is dry, cut it in half lengthwise. Now cut 2 holes in one of the halves for eyes. Paint the outer side of the mask and allow it to dry before decorating it with paper, paint, and any other media. Be sure to make holes on either side of the mask to attach pieces of yarn for ties around the head.

Purim mask.

Chapter 7

PASSOVER:
THE FESTIVAL OF FREEDOM

"... I am the Lord and I will bring you out from under
the burden of the Egyptians and I will deliver you from
their bondage. ..."

(Exodus 6:6)

As with the two other Jewish festivals, Sukkot and Shavuot, Passover serves a dual purpose. Its central theme is that of release—the Exodus from Egypt and the liberation of the Jewish people from bondage. It also has a seasonal theme—it marks the release from the cold of winter. Passover is a symbol of redemption not only for the Jewish people, but for the entire world. Today, Passover has become a time to remember those people all over the world who are oppressed and to give thanks for those who have been recently freed from suffering.

THE ORIGINS OF PASSOVER

Passover is an ancient holiday whose origins are deeply rooted in history. One of the oldest festivals in the world, *Pesah*, the predecessor to Passover, has been celebrated by Jews for more than three thousand years. In fact, Pesah was an established institution even before the Jews left Egypt!

The original Pesah ceremony was observed on the full moon of the first month of spring. At this ceremony, it was customary for every family to slaughter a lamb or goat at twilight. Once this was done, a bunch of hyssop was dipped in its blood and sprinkled on the doorpost and lintels of each house. Then, in the middle of the night, the slaughtered animal was eaten, along with unleavened bread and bitter herbs. It was necessary for the animal to be consumed in haste; any meat that was not eaten was to be burned before dawn. This ancient ceremony was called Pesah, but no one is quite sure why it was celebrated.

The celebration of Pesah coincided with the delivery of the Jews from Egypt. It was because the Hebrews sprinkled blood on their doorposts and lintels that God was

The seder plate contains: a lamb shank, greens, charoset, a toasted egg, and bitter herb.

This painting shows the moment in the seder when the door is opened to admit Elijah.

able to recognize and "pass over" his "chosen people," leaving them unscathed when he came to smite the first-born of the Egyptians—the last of the ten plagues (see page 102) visited upon the Jews' oppressors.

THE SEDER

The Passover *seder* (Hebrew for "order") re-creates the story of the Jews' flight from Egypt. It is a unique way of blending the past, present, and future into one experience. The Exodus from Egypt, while of great importance in itself, was also a very important catalyst, since it paved the way to Sinai and the deliverance of the Ten Commandments.

The Haggadah

The *Haggadah* is the book used during the seder to tell the story of the Exodus from Egypt, as well as to explore the meanings and complexities of the tale.

This custom has its roots in a scriptural command: "And thou shalt tell thy son in that day, saying: It is because of that which the Lord did to me when I came forth out of Egypt" (Exodus 13:8).

In the Haggadah are prayers, stories, and songs praising God for his help in leaving the bondage of Egypt. The Haggadah also contains words expressing the hope that one day all the peoples around the earth will be freed from their bondage, as well.

The Seder Plate

The principal feature of the seder is the eating of various foods associated with the departure from Egypt. Each of these foods is placed on a special plate—the seder plate—in the order in which it is used in the service, and each has a specific meaning and purpose. *Karpas*, or greens (often parsley), dipped in salt water, symbolize the coming of springtime, as well as hope and renewal. The greens are also reminders of the poor nourishment of the Israelites while in bondage, and the salt water is reminiscent of their tears. The *maror*, or bitter herb, usually consists of lettuce, horseradish, or endive and is eaten in remembrance of the affliction of slavery in Egypt. *Charoset*, made from apples, nuts, ginger, cinnamon, and wine and eaten on a piece of matzah, is prepared to resemble—in appearance—the mortar of the bricks the children of Israel used to build the cities of the Egyptian pharaoh Ramses. The *tzroa*, or shank bone of a lamb, commemorates the original Pesah ceremony. Finally, a *baytza*, or roasted egg, is placed on the plate as a symbol of rebirth and of the festival offering in the period of the Holy Temple. Three pieces of matzah, the unleavened bread also called the "bread of affliction," are placed on a separate covered plate. They serve as a remembrance of the quick flight from Egypt, when the Jews had no time to wait for their bread to rise and so baked it without yeast.

SEDER CUSTOMS

The Four Cups of Wine   During the ceremony, four cups of wine are to be drunk, commemorating the four verbs used in the act of redemption: "Wherefore I say unto the children of Israel: I am the Lord, and I will *bring* you out from under the burdens of the Egyptians, and I will *deliver* you from their bondage, and I will *redeem* you with an outstretched arm, and with great judgments; and I will *take* you unto Me for a people . . ." (Exodus 6:6–7).

The Cup of Elijah   A special cup of wine is poured before the seder begins for the prophet Elijah, who, it is

The youngest person at the seder recites the four questions.

said, will usher in messianic deliverance. He is believed to visit every Jewish home on the night of the seder. After the meal, one of the seder participants opens a door to admit Elijah.

The Four Questions   It is a Passover custom for the youngest person at the seder to ask: *"Why does this night differ from all other nights?"* and to recite the four questions, thus providing the leader of the seder with the opportunity to tell the Passover story in response. The questions are:

On all other nights we eat either leavened or unleavened bread; why on this night do we eat only unleavened bread?

On all other nights we eat all kinds of herbs; why on this night do we eat only bitter herbs?

On all other nights we need not dip our herbs even once; why on this night do we dip twice?

On all other nights we eat either sitting up or reclining; why on this night do we all recline?

This German kiddush cup from the late seventeenth century was created exclusively for use during Passover.

Reclining   A principal feature of the seder is the command to recline, symbolic of being free people who are able to eat with leisure.

The Ten Plagues   Ten plagues were sent down by God upon the Egyptians to show His wrath for the refusal of the pharaoh to release the children of Israel from bondage. During the seder it is customary to dip the pinkie finger into a glass of wine for each plague. They are: blood, frogs, lice, beasts, blight, boils, hail, locusts, darkness, and the slaying of the first-born.

Afikomen   A favored Passover custom is the hiding of the *afikomen*, half of one of the three pieces of matzah set aside early in the seder. Developed to keep the interest of the children, the afikomen is hidden during the meal by the leader of the seder. Later, the children are sent to look for it. All who participate in the search are given a prize, with a special prize awarded to the child who finds the afikomen. The afikomen is later shared by all at the table—the last thing eaten during the seder.

Of course, the afikomen is more than just a children's game. Symbolically, the tradition of the afikomen is thought by many to underscore the duality of Passover. The matzah half that remains on the seder table is pointed to often and plays an integral role as a catalyst for discussion during the seder. The hidden half, by this interpretation, stands for an individual's inner life.

The Matzah of Hope   A new custom is to set aside an extra piece of matzah, called the matzah of hope, for the Jews who are still oppressed in the Soviet Union.

Dayenu: We Should Have Been Content

This song praises God for all He did to help free the children of Israel from bondage.

How many of the claims of the Omnipresent upon our thankfulness!

Had He taken us out of Egypt, but not executed judgments on them,

> *We should have been content!*

Had He executed judgments on them but not upon their gods,

> *We should have been content!*

Had He executed judgments on their gods, but not slain their first-born,

> *We should have been content!*

Had He slain their first-born, but not given us their substance,

> *We should have been content!*

Had He given us their substance, but not torn the Sea apart for us,

> *We should have been content!*

Had he torn the Sea apart for us, but not brought us through it dry,

> *We should have been content!*

Had He brought us through it dry, but not sunk our oppressors in the midst of it,

> *We should have been content!*

Had He sunk our oppressors in the midst of it, but not satisfied our needs in the desert for forty years,

> *We should have been content!*

Had He satisfied our needs in the desert for forty years, but not fed us manna,

> *We should have been content!*

Had He fed us manna, but not given us the Sabbath,

> *We should have been content!*

Had He given us the Sabbath, but not brought us to Mount Sinai,

> *We should have been content!*

Had He brought us to Mount Sinai, but not given us the Torah,

> *We should have been content!*

Had He given us the Torah, but not brought us into the Land of Israel,

> *We should have been content!*

Had He brought us into the Land of Israel, but not built us the House of his choosing,

> *We should have been content!*

THE ARTISTIC TRADITION OF PASSOVER

Seder plates and matzah covers were central to the celebration of Passover. Therefore, many Jewish artists and craftsmen devoted their talents to creating beautiful objects of art to be used only for this festival. Seder plates made from gold, silver, copper, pewter, and earthenware, beautifully inscribed or engraved, have been found in all areas where Jews have lived; antique embroidered matzah covers, seder plates, and illuminated Haggadot are still used today.

These are illuminated Haggadot. The Haggadah on the left was created in 1300 in Spain. The Haggadah above was created in 1724 in Vienna.

The One Kid

This song is sung toward the end of the seder to keep the children interested. It alludes to Israel and the empires to which it was continually falling.

The one kid, the one kid, that daddy bought for two zuzim, the one kid, the one kid.

And the cat came and ate the kid, that daddy bought for two zuzim, the one kid, the one kid.

And the dog came and bit the cat, that ate the kid, that daddy bought for two zuzim, the one kid, the one kid.

And the stick came and beat the dog, that bit the cat, that ate the kid, that daddy bought for two zuzim, the one kid, the one kid.

And the fire came and burned the stick, that beat the dog, that bit the cat, that ate the kid, that daddy bought for two zuzim, the one kid, the one kid.

And the water came and put out the fire, that burned the stick, that beat the dog, that bit the cat, that ate the kid, that daddy bought for two zuzim, the one kid, the one kid.

And the ox came and drank up the water that put out the fire, that burned the stick, that beat the dog, that bit the cat, that ate the kid, that daddy bought for two zuzim, the one kid, the one kid.

And the butcher came, and butchered the ox, that drank up the water that put out the fire, that burned the stick, that beat the dog, that bit the cat, that ate the kid, that daddy bought for two zuzim, the one kid, the one kid.

And the Angel of Death came and slaughtered the butcher, who butchered the ox, that drank up the water that put out the fire, that burned the stick, that beat the dog, that bit the cat, that ate the kid, that daddy bought for two zuzim, the one kid, the one kid.

And the Holy One, blessed be He, came and slaughtered the Angel of Death, who slaughtered the butcher, who butchered the ox, that drank up the water that put out the fire, that burned the stick, that beat the dog, that bit the cat, that ate the kid, that daddy bought for two zuzim, the one kid, the one kid.

MENU: FOOD FOR THE PASSOVER SEDER

Matzah Ball Soup

Roasted Turkey Breast

Candied Carrots

Charoset (Chopped Apples, Dates, and Walnuts)

Steamed Asparagus

Sponge Cake with Strawberry Sauce

Matzah Balls

2 eggs, slightly beaten   ½ cup matzah meal
2 tablespoons corn oil   dash black pepper
2 tablespoons water

In a small bowl combine beaten eggs, corn oil, and water. Add matzah meal and pepper and blend well. Cover bowl and refrigerate for 20 minutes.

Meanwhile, fill a 4-quart pot with water and bring it to a boil. Reduce the heat slightly so water remains at a low boil. Using the hands, form balls of the matzah-meal mixture and drop the balls into the water. The balls will drop and then float. Cover the pot, lower the heat to medium-low, and cook the balls for 30 minutes.

When the balls are done, add them to chicken soup and serve. The recipe for Alphabet Chicken Soup (see page 21) can be used, but omit the alphabet noodles.

Yield: 8 matzah balls

Roasted Turkey Breast

turkey breast (4 to 5 pounds)

Place turkey breast in roasting pan in the oven. Roast for 2 hours at 325 degrees F or until meat thermometer registers 185 degrees F. Allow to cool slightly before slicing.

Yield: 12 servings

Candied Carrots

2 pounds carrots
1 cup brown sugar
2 tablespoons pareve margarine

Wash and scrape carrots and cut into ¼-inch-thick slices. Steam carrots for 20 to 30 minutes until tender. Drain and measure 1 cup of the cooking liquid. Add this liquid and the brown sugar and margarine to a pot. Bring to a boil, and stir until the margarine is melted and the sugar is dissolved, then turn down to simmer for 10 minutes. Add carrots and cook for 10 minutes.

Yield: 4 to 6 servings

Charoset

1 apple, quartered, cored, and peeled
½ cup finely chopped walnuts
¼ cup chopped dates
2 tablespoons honey
2 tablespoons sweet grape wine
½ teaspoon cinnamon

Finely chop apple and add to a small bowl. Add remaining ingredients and combine well.

Yield: 1¼ cups

Sponge cake with strawberry sauce.

Sponge Cake

> 7 eggs
> 1½ cups sugar
> 2 tablespoons lemon juice
> 1½ teaspoons lemon rind
> ¾ cup potato starch, sifted twice
> dash salt

Separate 6 of the eggs. Into a bowl with the 6 yolks, add the remaining whole egg and beat with an electric beater until light and fluffy. Gradually add the sugar, lemon juice, and lemon rind to the egg mixture. Beat constantly. Then add the potato starch and salt, also beating constantly.

Beat the 6 egg whites until stiff. Gently fold the beaten whites into the potato-starch mixture. Pour this slowly into an ungreased 10-inch tube pan (angel food pan). Bake at 350 degrees F for 50 minutes.

Invert cake and allow to cool in pan. Remove from pan when cool. Serve with Strawberry Sauce.

Yield: 1 sponge cake

Strawberry Sauce

> 1 pint fresh or frozen strawberries
> ¼ cup water
> 2 tablespoons sugar

Wash and hull strawberries if fresh. Add to a small pot with the water and bring to a boil. Cook several minutes. Then add to a blender with the sugar and purée.

Yield: 2 cups sauce

CRAFTS

Matzah Holder

Materials Needed:
2 pieces of fabric, 9 × 18 inches each
needle and thread

Fold and Sew:

First make a ½-inch hem on both 9-inch sides of each piece of fabric. Now lay the pieces on top of each other and fold the 18-inch sides exactly in half with the wrong side up. Hem another ½ inch on the 2 unfinished sides, sewing the 2 pieces together (4 layers of fabric will be in each seam). Turn it inside out and you've got 3 pockets for your matzah holder!

For Variety:

Use brightly colored or embroidered fabric to give your matzah cover a special touch.

Seder Plate

Materials Needed:
wax paper
rolling pin
self-hardening, non-firing clay (approximately 2 pounds)
plate large enough to hold 5 small dishes
knife
5 small dishes
felt
household cement

The Base:

Put wax paper down and roll out a large portion of the clay to about ¼ inch thick. Trace the plate onto it using a knife. Remove the plate and trim away excess clay. Use a little water whenever the clay needs to be smoothed out or is getting too dry to work with.

The Design:

Place the 5 dishes on the clay plate where you will want them to be when the plate is finished. Use more clay to roll long snakes as thick or thin as you like. Wind the snakes around the dishes to separate them. To attach the snakes to the clay plate, first remove the dishes. Then use the knife to make small X's on the part of the snake that will touch the clay plate and X's on the plate where the snake will touch it. Put a little water on the X's and put the snakes down.

Finishing Touch:

Allow the entire piece to dry (this may take a couple of days). Trace your clay plate onto a piece of felt. Trim the felt and glue it to the bottom of the clay plate with household cement. This will serve as a buffer between the clay plate and the table and will make the plate less fragile. Replace the 5 small dishes on the clay plate and fill with the symbolic foods of Passover.

Seder pillow.

Seder Pillow

Materials Needed:

> ¾ yard of 40-inch-wide fabric
> regular size pillow
> 3 yards of fringe or braid

Making a Pillow Sham:

Sew a 2-inch hem widthwise on the fabric. Wrap the fabric around the pillow. Make sure the fabric opening occurs in the middle of the back side of the pillow. Take the upper piece of fabric and fold it over the other piece (about 2 inches) to cover the opening and pin it into place.

Sewing:

Remove the pillow from the fabric and turn the fabric inside out. Sew 1-inch seams on both unfinished sides to secure the envelope you've created. With the front side up, baste the fringe or braid around the edges.

Embroidering:

If you'd like to decorate your pillow, use embroidery. See figure 1 for a suggestion.

Figure 1

Chapter 8

SHAVUOT: THE FESTIVAL OF WEEKS

"You shall observe the Feast of Weeks for the Lord your God, offering your freewill contribution according as the Lord your God has blessed you."

Deuteronomy 16:10

The third and final Jewish festival of the year, Shavuot, meaning "weeks" in Hebrew, is so named because it is celebrated seven weeks after Passover. As with the two other festivals, Sukkot and Passover, Shavuot has both a spiritual and an agricultural meaning. It commemorates the anniversary of the giving of the Ten Commandments on Mount Sinai; it is also named *Hag Hakatsir*, the harvest festival, and *Hag Habikurim*, the festival of first fruits.

Shavuot differs from the two other festivals in that a specific historical observance is not mentioned in the Torah; it was only later tradition that identified it with Moses and Sinai. In the Torah, it is written that the "Israelites shall hold a festival for the Feast of the harvest, of the first fruits of your work, of what you sow in the field" (Exodus 23:16), but there is no mention of the connection between the giving of the law and any specific observance or celebration.

Shavuot lasts only two days, yet has great significance—it celebrates the special relationship between God and man, and reaffirms every Jew's commitment to a life of study and religious practice. For this reason, young Jewish adults, who have already been *bar* or *bat mitzvahed*, are "confirmed" on this holiday. That is, they reaffirm their commitment to Judaism and to the Jewish people in a service that is the highlight of the spiritual observance of the festival. The service is particularly important because the dedicated young people represent the hope and promise of tomorrow.

In Israel, the holiday takes on a more agrarian tone. At this time, the winter wheat is harvested—bearing the first fruits of the year. Special dairy meals are prepared using the fruits of the harvest.

Shavuot and Passover are interconnected holidays. Both are related to the grain harvest, and both are intertwined with the receiving of the Torah on Mount Sinai. On Passover, Jews thank God for the act of freeing them from slavery. The release from slavery eventually allowed the Jews to receive the Torah—which is the reason that Shavuot is celebrated.

This painting by Marc Chagall celebrates the giving of the Ten Commandments.

Traditionally, there were two sacrifices to be made on Shavuot: two loaves of bread brought to the temple in Jerusalem and offered to God and a freewill offering brought by every family according to its means. These sacrifices were brought from the first fruits of the season: wheat, barley, grapes, figs, pomegranates, olives, and dates.

SHAVUOT CUSTOMS

One Shavuot custom is to stay up all night studying and discussing the Torah. There are two reasons for this. The first is that because the Israelites fell asleep the night before receiving the Torah and had to be awakened by Moses, we now stay up all night to show our eagerness for receiving the law. It is also said that the heavens open up at midnight on Shavuot, making it an auspicious time for prayers and thoughts to ascend to heaven and be heard.

Decorating the home and synagogue with greens and fresh flowers is another Shavuot custom. This serves as a reminder of the ancient practice of bringing the first fruits to the temple in Jerusalem and calls to mind our hopes for an abundant harvest. Many synagogues spread grass on the floor of the synagogue as a symbol of the foliage that covered Mount Sinai when Moses received the Ten Commandments. It is also customary to weave a crown of flowers and branches and place it upon the Torah. *Shavuoslech*, or "little Shavuots," are related to this custom; these papercuts were created and used instead of the actual greenery.

The Book of Ruth is customarily read on Shavuot. It tells the story of a woman who willingly accepts Judaism, in much the same way that the Jewish people willingly accepted the Torah from God. She says: "Wither thou goest, I will go . . . and thy god will be my God" (Ruth 1:16).

THE SECOND DAY

Outside of Israel and reformed congregations, two days of Shavuot are celebrated. According to tradition, King David was born and died on this second day, so a candle is lit for him and a memorial service is held. The prayer memorializes deceased friends and relatives as well as the martyrs of both previous and present generations.

FOOD

It is customary to eat dairy dishes on Shavuot. Many explanations are given for this: There is an analogy between the sweetness and physical nourishment the Jew receives from milk and honey and the spiritual nourishment gained from the reading of the Torah. Meat is not eaten because it may serve as a reminder of the golden calf—something that should not be thought about because it led to the breaking of the tablets of the Ten Commandments.

Twin challot are baked on Shavuot, representing the two tables of the Ten Commandments and the two loaves of bread traditionally offered to God in the era of the first temple. As it is written: "You shall bring from your settlements two loaves of bread as a wave of offering . . . baked after leavening, as first fruits to the Lord" (Leviticus 23:17).

It is a custom of Shavuot to stay up all night studying the Torah.

MENU: FOOD FOR SHAVUOT

Spring Sorrel Soup

Cheese Blintzes

Fresh Raspberry Sauce

Lightly Steamed and Marinated Sugar Snap Peas

Poppy Seed Pound Cake

Fresh Fruit

Spring Sorrel Soup

1 pound sorrel (Schav) or sour grass (see note)
6 cups boiling water
1 onion, chopped
1 tablespoon vegetable oil
1 egg
½ teaspoon salt
1 tablespoon sugar
½ cup sour cream
½ cup finely chopped cucumber or
   1 hard-cooked egg, finely chopped

Wash the sorrel carefully, remove the stems, and set aside. Chop the leaves, add them to the boiling water, and cook for 20 minutes. In a separate pot, cook the chopped stems in a cup of water for 20 minutes. (When done they will be soft and will have absorbed all the water.) Mash the stems through a sieve and put this into the pot of cooking leaves.

Sauté the chopped onion in the oil until golden and add this to the leaves. When the leaves have finished cooking, beat the egg in a small bowl. Add ¼ cup of the cooking liquid to the beaten egg, whisking continuously. Add another ½ cup of the hot liquid, continually beating the egg mixture. Now add the egg mixture to the soup and beat well. Add the salt and sugar to the soup and stir. Allow the soup to cool and then refrigerate until serving.

To serve, spoon the cold soup into a bowl and garnish with a dollop of sour cream and a tablespoon of chopped cucumber or chopped hard-cooked egg.

Yield: 6 servings

Note: If sorrel is not available, spinach can be used with the addition of 2 tablespoons of lemon juice to achieve the sour flavor.

Cheese Blintzes

3 eggs   ⅓ cup unbleached flour
¼ cup milk   1 tablespoon butter
¼ cup water

Add eggs to a small bowl and beat well with a wire whisk. Add milk and water to the eggs and beat again. Add the flour to the mixture, slowly, beating continuously as the flour is added. A smooth and thin mixture will result.

Heat a 7-inch sauté pan over medium heat until hot. Add about a teaspoon of butter or margarine. When this has melted, add about 2 tablespoons of the batter and tilt the pan until the batter has covered the bottom. Heat the batter until it begins to cook and the edges curl away from the sides of the pan. Invert the pan over a clean dish towel that has been spread out over a counter or on a table. The cooked crêpe should fall easily out of the pan.

When all the crêpes are prepared, the filling can be made.

Yield: 12 crêpes

Cheese Filling

12 to 16 ounces dry-curd low-fat cottage cheese
1 tablespoon sugar
1 tablespoon butter

Pour off any liquid from the top of the cottage cheese and place the cottage cheese in a small bowl. Add the sugar and combine well.

To fill the blintzes, place a crêpe on a plate with the cooked side up. Place a tablespoon of the cottage cheese filling in the center of the crêpe. Fold the 2 sides over the cottage cheese and then turn the bottom up over the cheese and then the top up over the cheese like an envelope. Fill all 12 crêpes.

To complete the cooking, sauté each blintz in butter until golden brown on both sides. This can be done in a large saucepan using about a tablespoon of butter. Serve the blintzes with sour cream, low-fat sour cream, apple sauce, or fruit purées.

Yield: Filling for 12 blintzes

Fresh Raspberry Sauce

1 pint raspberries
2 tablespoons sugar (optional)

Mash berries in Foley food mill and press the berry pulp and liquid through the mill to eliminate the seeds. Combine the purée with sugar if you wish. Serve immediately.

Yield: 2 cups

Cheese blintzes with fresh raspberry sauce.

Lightly Steamed and Marinated Sugar Snap Peas

3 cups sugar snap peas
2 tablespoons red wine vinegar
1 tablespoon olive oil
1 teaspoon chopped fresh basil
greens
2 scallions, finely sliced

Steam sugar snap peas until tender, about 3 to 5 minutes. Drain and add to a bowl. Toss with wine vinegar, olive oil, and basil.

Arrange greens on salad plates. Top with sugar snap peas and then some finely sliced scallions.

Yield: 4 servings

Poppy Seed Pound Cake

1 cup butter or margarine	½ teaspoon baking soda
1½ cups sugar	⅔ cup sour cream or yogurt
4 eggs	⅔ cup poppy seeds
2¼ cups cake flour	1 teaspoon vanilla

Spray a 9 × 5-inch loaf pan with a non-stick spray. In a large bowl, cream the butter or margarine. Add the sugar and beat until fluffy. Add the eggs, one at a time, and beat well.

In another bowl, combine the flour and baking soda. Add this mixture to the butter mixture alternately with the sour cream or yogurt. Add the poppy seeds and the vanilla. Pour this batter into the 9 × 5-inch pan and bake at 300 degrees F for 1½ hours.

Cool in pan for 10 minutes and then remove from pan and allow to cool.

Yield: 10 servings

Lightly steamed and marinated sugar snap peas.

Figure 1

CRAFTS

Macrame Hanging Plant

Materials Needed:

    4 pieces twine, each 5 yards long   **large beads**
    3-inch ring   **scissor**

To Begin:

Cut 4 5-yard lengths of twine. Fold each piece in half and attach them to the ring by pulling their ends through the ring and the loop at the top of the folded twine (see figure 1).

The Stitch:

There is really only one stitch needed for this project; variations of it will provide enough ways to make your macrame more interesting. The square knot stitch is simple and is done with 4 pieces of string or twine. The 2 pieces in the middle never move. Take the piece on the right and loosely cross the other 3 with it. Take the twine from the left and put it on top of the crossed twine and

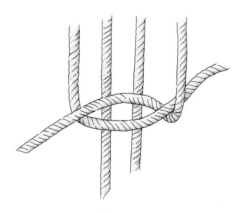

Figure 2

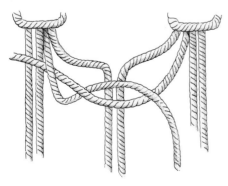

Figure 3

then cross the other 2 from underneath. Now put the same thread through the hole made by crossing the right piece. Pull on the side threads to tighten the knot (see figure 2). Repeat the same process from the other side.

Variations:

1. If the knot is made from 1 side only, it will produce a spiralling effect.
2. If the square knot is made with neighboring threads, it will link them together (see figure 3).
3. Add beads and continue working knots around them.

To Continue and End:

Using any combination of the stitches described, work evenly and neatly until there's no less then 1 foot of twine unworked. Make square knots, a few inches down, with neighboring threads. Now, gather all of the ends together and make a big half-knot at the bottom. A plant should rest nicely on this knot.

Macrame hanging plant.

Photographs by Michael Grand pp. 20, 22, 23, 24, 27, 38, 40, 41, 48, 50, 51, 52, 54, 55, 57, 66, 68, 70, 71, 78, 80, 81, 82, 90, 92, 93, 94, 95, 106, 108, 109, 110, 111, 112, 120, 122, 123, 125

With other contributions from:
p. 12   The Jewish Museum/Art Resource, New York; p. 13   "Shabbat Meal", The Jewish Theological Seminary of America; pp. 14–15   © A. Gurmankin/Unicorn Stock Photos; p. 16   © Mary Ann Evans; p. 17   The Jewish Museum/Art Resource, New York; p. 18   © Bernice Jones; p. 19   The Jewish Museum/Art Resource, New York; p. 32   Menkes, "Reading of the Torah," The Jewish Museum/Art Resource, New York; p. 33   Scala/Art Resource, New York; p. 34   © Richard Lobell; p. 35   The Jewish Museum/Art Resource, New York; p. 36   The Jewish Theological Seminary of America; p. 37   The Jewish Theological Seminary of America; p. 44   The Jewish Theological Seminary of America; p. 45   The Jewish Museum/Art Resource, New York; pp. 46–47   The Jewish Theological Seminary of America; p. 61   The Jewish Museum/Art Resource, New York; p. 62   The Jewish Museum/Art Resource, New York; p. 63   © Richard Lobell; p. 64   The Jewish Museum/Art Resource, New York; p. 65   The Jewish Theological Seminary of America; p. 74   © Bernice Jones; p. 75   The Jewish Museum/Art Resource, New York; p. 76   © Melabee Miller/Envision; p. 86   The Jewish Museum/Art Resource, New York; p. 87   The Jewish Museum/Art Resource, New York; pp. 88–89   Mimi Gross, Purim Masks, The Jewish Museum/Art Resource, New York; p. 98   © Bernice Jones; p. 99   Raisa Robbins, "Passover Night," The Jewish Theological Seminary of America; pp. 100–101   The Jewish Theological Seminary of America; p. 102   The Jewish Museum/Art Resource, New York; p. 104   The Jewish Theological Seminary of America; p. 105   The Jewish Theological Seminary of America; pp. 116–117   Richard Lobell; p. 119   © A. Gurmankin/Unicorn Stock Photos